Website Valuation

How to calculate the worth of a website

Paul Haarman

Table of Contents

Chapter 1:
What is a website?

- Online real estate
- Location, location, location
- What determines a location good or bad?
- The backstreets and avenues of the internet
- What makes a website great?
- The hidden forces of a website
- The difference between a website and an online shop

Chapter 2:
When is a website valuation needed?

- Selling a website
- Buying a website
- Investing in an existing website
- Mergers and acquisitions
- Financing and credit
- Bankruptcy, restructuring and restart
- Personal problems between owners

Chapter 3:
Why a pure financial valuation will not do?

- But is the performance of our website not included in our results?
- Why multiplying historic results will not do the trick

- Using a financial valuation as a starting point

Chapter 4:
Components of a website valuation method

- What factors determine the value of a website?
- The 5 website value drivers
- And what about the financial results up to now?
- The process of valuing a website

Chapter 5:
The 5 website value drivers

- Why do these 5 elements drive value?
- Organic traffic strength
- Online authority strength
- Technical Strength
- Advertising & social strength
- Conversion strength

Chapter 6:
Weighing the 5 website value drivers

- Explaining cause and effect through analyzing data
- Comparing the strength of our 5 website value drivers
- Combining intensity and duration of impact
- Calculating the weighting factor of each website value driver

Chapter 7:
The website valuation process

- Step 1: Financial valuation
- Step 2: Deciding on the weighting factors of the 5 website value drivers
- When could weighting factors deviate from the average aggregated factors?
- Step 3: Assessing the relative strength of each website value driver
- Step 4: Adding a multiplier to each website value driver
- Step 5: Calculating the final worth of a website

Chapter 8:

Financial valuation methods and challenges

- Attribution of sales, profits and costs
- Attribution challenges for ecommerce websites
- Attribution challenges for non-ecommerce websites
- What are the main challenges?
- So how to use hard data in our financial valuation?
- The impact of less qualitative financial data on the valuation process
- How do I go about adjusting the weight of the financial valuation process?
- A large choice of financial valuation methods
- Income based methods
    1. Discounted Cash Flow method
    2. Capitalization of Earnings method
- Asset based methods
- Market based methods
- Rules of Thumb
- So what to choose?
- What if no financial data is available?

Chapter 9:

Website valuation in practice

- Our case
- Financial valuation
- Qualitative valuation
- Organic strength calculation
- Online authority strength calculation
- Advertising & social media strength calculation
- Conversion strength calculation
- Technical strength calculation
- Calculating the total weighted multiplier
- Final website valuation

Chapter 10:
Valuing a website without ecommerce activities

- The attribution method
    1. Valuing and attributing the current money stream
    2. Financial valuation
    3. Assessing the strength of the 5 website value drivers
- The possible buyer method
    1. What would a possible buyer be willing to pay
    2. Estimating the worth of your organic traffic
    3. Estimating the worth of your online authority

Chapter 11:
Flow chart website valuation

Chapter 12:
Pitfalls of website valuations

- Bot traffic
- Paid traffic

- Iceberg websites
- Financial results
- Pressure from your client

Chapter 13:

What about the value of domains?

- The worth of empty domains without a website
- The worth of a domain with a website built around

Chapter 14:

Websites as online real estate

- Ecommerce websites vs physical shops
- Non-ecommerce websites vs commercial real estate
- The implications of regarding websites as online real estate
    1. Impact on business owners and general management
    2. Impact on accounting and taxation
    3. Impact on investments and investors

Chapter 15:

Acquiring a website

- Browse through some website market places
- Large acquisitions require a team of specialists
- Discuss your plans before acquisition
- Work on your newly acquired website
- Make your own calculations regarding the asking price
- Negotiate with knowledge
- There is no certainty in acquisitions

Chapter 16:

The future of retailing and website acquisitions

- An acquisition driven market
- The impact of the Amazon's and Alibaba's of this world
- The future of online retailing
- And what about physical stores and omni channel strategies?
- The evolution of the market for website valuations
- Changing the M&A market
- Use your brain power!

About the author

My name is Paul Haarman, a digital marketing consultant and digital M&A consultant with a broad interest in entrepreneurship, investing and business development. I studied Marketing at HEAO Business School and Business Economics at Erasmus University Rotterdam, The Netherlands. My company is based in The Netherlands but currently I am living in Belgium.

Since 1999 I have operated several online activities on my own. Some of these were concentrated around websites based upon advertising and affiliate models, some were businesses with a mix of online and off line activities. During the last 15 years I have helped many large and medium-sized companies with their digital strategy.

In 2012 I became aware of the difficulties companies were struggling with in valuing their digital activities. I went through hundreds of analytical reports and performed many statistical probes to reach the core of the website engines that drive value. Then I tried to come up with a general method of determining the worth of a website or digital activity. In this book you will read all about it.

My opinion is that we are entering a new phase of the internet where acquisitions of websites and digital companies will become the new frontier of digital business. It will be an alternative strategy to building an online presence on your own, especially when the latter will become harder and more expensive to achieve and increases the risk of lower returns on investments that also will take up more time to materialize.

Copyright © 2018 – 2019 Paul Haarman

Published by: Intellect Investments BV, Smederijstraat 2, 4814 DB BREDA, The Netherlands

All rights reserved. No portion of this book may be reproduced in any form without permission of the publisher.

www.webworthpartners.com

Why this book?

Every idea begins with inspiration. Sometimes inspiration comes in the form of a sentence you read in a book or on a blogpost, sometimes it is something said by a person you never have met before. In other cases it just grows on you as you are confronted with practical challenges that somehow need an answer. For me the idea of building a website valuation method was inspired by a myriad of inspirations. Before inspiration is able to do its fruitful work you need a mindshift. For me this mindshift occurred when I saw one of my websites becoming a market leader. During the course of a couple of years this website grew with double digits in traffic and results and it kept on growing. It was not only the market that drove results, it was the inner engine of the website that kept it growing. I saw with my own eyes that a website was an entity on its own, not merely a marketing channel. It vested its own place on the streets of the internet, I regarded it as online real estate.

In my day-to-day work as an online marketing and digital M&A consultant I have seen websites and online shops grow from scratch to very successful lead- and sales generating entities. I also witnessed firsthand the pain and effort that it takes to turn a website or online shop into a money making machine, an almost unstoppable engine, creating new sales and profits due to the inner strength of the website itself.

After this mindshift that took place in 2006 - 2011 it took me a couple of years to establish the method of website valuation I will discuss in this book. I was (and still am) an online marketing consultant with many years of experience in SEO and Google Ads campaigns. In the span of more than 15 years I have given advice to hundreds of national and international companies regarding their online marketing strategy. Due to my work I saw how the authority of a website manifested itself through optimizations in website content, technical advancements, a better understanding of using online advertising tools and conversion optimizations.

I also learned that in order to value a website or online shop it did not suffice to look back on the financial results it had achieved in previous years. There were other forces at play, still hiding behind the tangible results of financial results, that were propelling a website towards results in the future. Eventually this led to a method that would honor these forces. From 2013 on I began working and experimenting with a method to establish the real worth of a website. I will not bother you with the initial mistakes and wrong lines of thought I pursued. It took me a year to construct a method that was both practical and logical. In 2014 I began valuating websites as a side-service of my own online marketing business. I published some articles on the web that attracted customers who were in the middle of buying or selling websites and they were all too glad to have found an appraiser specialized in websites and online shops. It appeared I was the only one that was really set out to professionally guide online entrepreneurs in establishing the worth of a website.

In the last couple of years I have made many valuations of websites and ecommerce websites using my method. Now it is time to share this method as I am convinced that there really is a demand for a method of website valuation that can be used for almost each and every website no matter its market, origin or use.

So why this book? Because I think there is a need, and an increasing one as more and more websites are being sold, often based upon the wrong or limited foundations of valuation. There is a market, and a growing one as the internet has become a battlefield of websites and shops competing for customers were the limits of organic growth are in sight. Consolidation is in many cases a better option for growth than trying to grow your own digital entities.

More importantly, the M&A market is changing rapidly as digital becomes an integral part of doing business. The digital presence of a company is a strategic asset that is gaining more and more importance day by day. Whether acquiring or selling a pure online player or a more traditional business, its digital strategy will affect its value. Understanding this value is what this book is all about.

It's the people, stupid!

Because digital is not about data, it is about people. The people that connect to a company, the people that are customers, the people that may become customers, the people that talk about your business and brand, the authority they give you, believing that what you say is true and important. In this book I will show you a way to value a website based upon 5 important qualitative characteristics that will be quantified leading to a value in money. But do not be fooled about money. Even valuations are not about money, money is only a transferrable entity. Each and every company's value is based upon how they help people, the solutions they bring and how people see and reward a company for now and in the future.

Chapter 1: What is a website?

Let us begin with the most fundamental question. What is a website?
Is it an online presentation of your company? Is it a communication channel to your target audience? Is it an expression of your thoughts and ideas? Is it a shop? It may be all of the above and much more. But in essence it is an asset. It is something we have created and cared for. It is serviced, updated, fitted to new needs, expanded with fresh content and features and embellished with graphics and pictures. We build it, renovate it and enlarge it. It is just like a house, an office or a shop. It is online real estate.

Online real estate
Just like brick and mortar real estate, a website needs attention and additional investments to keep it up to date. Your web designers, online marketing consultants, SEO specialists and advertising agencies are your subcontractors that help it to flourish and prosper. When built and cared for the right way it will give you a return on your investment. It will bring in readers, subscribers, leads, sales and interactions, whatever you are looking for. If you neglect it the goals you pursue will falter or not materialize at all and eventually your investments will evaporate.

Location, location, location
What is the essence of real estate? You cannot move it. It is attached to a specific place on a specific street in a specific region. You may change the structure, renovate the roof or remodel the interior but it will stay put in the same location. The worth of real estate is very much depended upon its location. Your house or shop may be as beautiful and

spacious as your dreamhouse, but when it is situated in the wrong location you will probably not buy it nor even come and take a look at it. A poorly maintained house in a great location or a small shop in the best shopping street of a city will always attract buyers. That is why the mantra "Location, Location, Location" is so embedded in the minds and hearts of successful real estate developers. They know that the bulk of the real estate's worth in the future will be depended upon the right location. The same goes for bankers and renters. Banks will provide higher mortgages for the same building constructed in a prime location compared to a lower ranked location. Shop renters will pay higher rents on smaller shops in upscale shopping streets.

What determines a location good or bad?

In real estate there are many location factors that may influence the qualification good or bad.

Let's name a few for shops:

- Number of shopping traffic
- Average income of shoppers
- Proximity of city center
- Car park availability
- Proximity of railway or subway station
- History of the street
- Quality of surrounding shops
- Proximity of restaurants

These are all more or less tangible factors albeit qualitative ones. On either location factor considered you could have a discussion. Still the name of a specific street will automatically attach feelings of location to it.

Not so with websites, there is not one street or location, there are thousands of them. And still you can attach a ranking of location to a single website varying from bad to excellent. We don't call it location however, we call it organic search strength and online authority.

The backstreets and avenues of the internet

The best thing about a website is that you can build it, expand it and move it. You can go from a website with 100 visitors a month to one with 100.000 visitors a month. It may take some time and effort (or money of course) but all is possible. How do you attract visitors? You must be visible on one or more streets of the internet. Each and every search query forms a street were the top result is in the most visible spot. These streets may be long and just like other fine shopping streets in the physical world they will get shabbier and cheaper at the ends were only a few shoppers want (or dare) to go. Social media like Facebook and YouTube also form online streets were you may be noticed or totally ignored.

The real issue here is that your website may pop up on many streets or just a handful. It may be prominent on minor streets but invisible on large avenues and it may be omnipresent on every single street that is relevant to your business. I can tell you, it makes a big difference what your online locations are.

Will a website with great visibility be able to attract more customers, leads, sales or whatever you want? For sure! Is a website with a presence on more and better online streets more worth than a website that is almost invisible? You bet!

These were the easy questions. Let's try some more challenging ones.

Are organic streets (through SEO) more valuable than paid streets (through online advertising)? Yes they are! Traffic from organic streets is free, has a high quality and, even more importantly, organic streets are reasonably stable. A website that scores well on some search queries will in general do that for many years to come. Maybe even more important: a website that is able to take up prominent positions on organic streets stands a better chance in popping up at other organic locations. The internet is above all a winner-takes-all environment.

Let's say your website is on the move. Organic traffic growth is substantial, your news articles are picked up by a growing audience on Facebook, your Google Ads campaign is getting more and more profitable and your conversion rate is climbing. In other words you are moving up on the social ladder of the internet. And right at this moment you receive a call from an outside investor who wants to buy your website. Will you sell yourself short if you would take the results up to now as the basis for a website valuation? Yes, you will. An important part of the strength of your website has not materialized yet into the results up to this moment.

Here is a big difference with offline real estate. Your physical location will not improve significantly over time (in fact with physical real estate the chances of locations deteriorating are bigger). The same goes for shops located in a busy shopping street. The street may get a bit busier but this has mostly nothing to do with the street but more with the economy and consumer spending power, outside factors that cannot be assigned to the strength of the shop. But with websites and online shops this strength is already present within the website, it only needs time to materialize.

What would happen if you would stop working on your website right now? Will it still attract visitors to your website content? Oh, for sure! And if a robot would send out your products presented on your online shop, orders would still come in. What happens when you close the door of your physical shop? Nothing? That would be too optimistic, people stop buying from day 1 and they will not be coming back easily when it would re-open again after a few months.

What makes a website great?

I often get this question. "What do you think of my website"? In most cases I am asked this question when someone has made a new website or when I first meet a new customer who wants to hear my opinion about his or her website. By looking at a website I will see its design and when I go through some pages I can tell if an effort has been made to attract and engage visitors. By spending some more time I can judge whether the website is designed to convert visitors into customers or followers. That is all great, but it will not tell me if I am looking at a mediocre website or a superb one. Of course, a truly great website will have website content that attracts people and it also will have a fine way of making customers or fans. But there are numerous websites out there that I do not find good looking but are really superb websites with great online results. Beauty is in the eye of the beholder and I have learned to dismiss this aspect of a website when people ask me about their website. The funny thing is that in most cases people expect me to comment on the design.

So what is a good or great website? It is a website or online shop that attracts a large chunk of organic traffic that is interested in what the website has to offer. It is a website that is seen as an authority in its field. It is a website that pops up in many streets of the internet. It is a website that functions well on all devices and let people navigate through its content in a clear and logic way. It is also a website that is great in turning visitors into customers, followers or fans. In short, it is a website that gets results and a truly great website will show progress in all these traits.

The hidden forces of a website

What you see is not always what you get. That goes for all things in life, even with people. It's the same with websites. A website may be looking great, but will it perform well? And even more importantly, will it keep on performing in the future? By looking at the results of today and yesterday we will get a picture of its performance. But in order to understand the strength of a website we will have to look a bit deeper. Where are these results coming from and what will they tell you about future results?

In this book I will explore these hidden forces that really are the driving forces of a website or online shop. Luckily they are not that hidden after all. We can detect them and we can calculate them although the outcome will never be a 100% mathematical result. But that is never the case with valuations. By unearthing and qualifying these forces we will get a better understanding of the engine of a website and we will be able to gauge whether this engine will be able to drive up results even more or that chances are that this engine will falter.

The difference between a website and an online shop

In this book I will use the term website in general, also referring to online shops. Here I will discuss the difference, viewed from our focal point in determining its worth.

An online shop or ecommerce website is a website where products or services can be bought online. There is a shopping cart, payment options and you can buy your products or services right away. An online shop is a transaction-oriented website. Most pages of an online shop are filled with products or services to buy.

A general information-based website is not aimed at direct transactions. Most pages or all pages provide information or backgrounds or even news. It is aimed at other conversions: leads, subscriptions, followers, clicks on advertisements and many more softer goals.

Of course there are hybrid websites. Most news websites do have an online shop incorporated where you can subscribe and pay for your subscription. It does not make it an online shop. The bulk of the pages is about news and stories.

We talked about websites as being online real estate. But with an online shop it is even more than that. It also is pure transaction-based business. You are investor and shopkeeper at the same time. Your online shop should be visible on many solid online locations but it also must provide the ultimate shopping experience aimed at transactions.

For our purpose of establishing the worth of a website it makes a big difference whether we are dealing with a pure ecommerce website or with an information-based website. With an online shop we can calculate with direct sales and profits. With an information-based website the biggest challenge is to calculate the value added by the website in terms of sales and profits. I have come across company websites aimed at lead conversions that administer leads to sales conversions in a pretty proper way. In other situations the challenge was much more difficult when no direct attributions could be made from website visits to leads or sales. The latter is common at websites that generate the bulk of its leads through telephone calls.

In this book we will come up with different approaches of valuations for online shops and information-based websites although the general line of thought is similar.

Chapter 2: When is a website valuation needed?

When you start to see your website as an investment that enables you to make sales and profits it is easy to understand that your website has a value. Here we will explore situations when that value becomes important. In my experience as a website valuator I have come across many situations where there was a need for establishing the worth of a website.

Selling a website
In many cases it is the selling party that is interested in establishing the worth of a website or online shop. Reasons for selling may vary widely but from my experience I can say that in many cases website owners are approached by interested buying parties and this makes them wonder what a good asking price may be.
The main purpose for a selling party to get a website valuation is asking the right price and not selling oneself short.

Buying a website
Of course buying parties also have a major interest in knowing what they buy. Buying parties are becoming more and more active in their search for websites that will add value to their business model. We are entering an era where the cost of organic growth or growth through advertising is becoming more expensive every year. This will trigger a buying market for websites and online shops.

Some buying parties are actively searching for websites that will suit their needs. In some cases they focus on websites within their territory that attract lots of organic traffic. This is especially true for parties that intend to grow their business exponentially without having to invest time and money in their own website. Do not forget that organic traffic does not come in overnight and buying your way into the market through online advertising may be much more expensive than buying the traffic from an existing website. What most of these buyers have in place is a very well-functioning monetizing model. They either have an online shop or they sell a single product and service that matches the target audience of the website they are interested in. In most cases they are looking for information-based websites that are in general much better than online shops in triggering loads of organic traffic. Besides, in buying an information-based website they will not have to pay for the sales generated by the online shop, they only are after the traffic.

Another market segment of buyers are the online shop owners that want to buy similar online shops. They too are confronted with the choice of growing their own online shop or buying traffic and sales through the shop of their competitors. Here the calculation is not only based upon the cost of growing their own shop relative to the cost of acquisition. Another important asset of such a deal is that you eliminate one of your competitors. With the rising costs of organic growth and online advertising costs I expect that this type of growth through acquisition will explode in the coming years.

There is another buying market going on, also mainly within the world of online shops. From an online marketing point of view it is not a very wise strategy to add new product categories to your online shop. By doing that you will hamper your SEO strategy (as more focused websites may be higher ranked than general players) and you will lose your niche in the market. Customers do not always like to see their favorite shop turning itself in a department store. For online entrepreneurs who want to diversify it makes plain and simple sense to buy another online shop within another market niche. They know how to run an online shop profitable, they have been through the process of optimization and they can add their know-how to an existing online shop. Again, in most cases a better alternative than beginning from scratch.

The main purpose of a website valuation for a buying party is almost the same as for the selling party: understanding its worth and not paying too much.

Investing in an existing website

Websites and online shops need to grow to keep ahead of competition. But growing may require additional assets. That is why there is a market for external investors that are interested in putting up the money in exchange of a piece of ownership of the website or online shop. But what are they buying into? And what amount of investment corresponds with which piece of the pie of the website? It all boils down in establishing a website worth that all parties may confide in.

There is a lot of investment going on in online startups. But in second or third financing rounds a valuation of the already functioning online proposition is needed. In most cases the proposition of startups is centered around a website with visitors, conversions and subscriptions, whatever the unique proposition may be. Valuing the proposition is valuing the website, this is the place where all things come together.

The main purpose of valuation for investors and current owners will be calculating the website worth as a starting point for negotiations about money invested and agreed returns or shares issued.

Mergers and acquisitions

In many businesses the company website plays a central role in the day-to-day operations of a company. Think of lead generation, customer communications, product communications and news updates. The company website is the market place of a company where potential and existing customers are browsing through information, product pages and news. In the world of mergers and acquisitions it is essential that all value and asset components will be taken into account. Looking only at financial data will not tell the whole story. A specific valuation of the website would be beneficial to all parties involved.

Many companies in both B2C and B2B markets operate one or more online shops, in most cases additional to the corporate information-based website. When that is the case an appraisal of the digital presence is even more important.

What both buying and selling parties need is a clear understanding of assets that will be transferred. The value of the website(s) should be included next to assets as physical real estate and inventory .

Financing and credit

Credit and financing go hand in hand with valuations. Here the central question is what the collateral is as security for the bank or investment company providing the loan or financing arrangement. It all depends on the company, the purpose of financing and the actual financial report whether an appraisal is needed.

Imagine an ecommerce company growing fast but in need of cash to expand further. A financial review will give some data but not all, maybe sales are booming but profits are still negative. What to look for to back a credit apply? Of course assets will give substance. An online shop with a high online authority and a load of fans and followers may be the collateral banks need to approve the credit extension. Let's not forget that many of our highly ranked ecommerce businesses do not make solid profits yet but that does not make them less valuable. You only have to look at their stock market value to see that investors look for other traits to value them.

Bankruptcy, restructuring and restart

When a company is going downhill there comes a time to consider options. Going bankrupt is one of these options, restructuring or making a restart after bankruptcy are others to consider. In many cases outside investors or third parties like banks or investors will get involved in this difficult process. In order to make sound decisions one needs to know what the state of existing assets is. In today's online world it may just be that the website or online shop may be the item that attracts the most attention. For restructuring purposes an underperforming online strategy may give investors and owners the incentive to try a new approach.

When bankruptcy is unavoidable and the company is drawn into receivership one will look at assets to be sold. Real estate and websites are the first they will go for. But what will the company website(s) be worth? A crucial question in order to obtain the best possible price for creditors.

When a restart is considered outside investors often will join the table entering a phase of investing and deliberation. Again questions about assets will have to be met.

Personal problems between owners

Whenever you are in business with one or more partners tensions may appear. Sometimes these tensions will lead to break-ups. It is all up to the owners themselves whether this break-up will be executed in a thoughtful and considerate manner. What will help is an objective and substantiated valuation of the assets involved. When the digital component of the company is large it is evident that a website valuation will be part of this process.

Chapter 3: Why a pure financial valuation will not do?

What is wrong with a valuation based upon financial results? Well, nothing of course. The problem is that it will only tell part of the story and in some cases, particularly in fast growing online environments, it will tell you nothing.

When a valuation is needed for a going concern with a history of financial results and asset values that may be deduced from the financial reports a pure financial valuation will do just fine. When focusing on the financial track record a thorough view of a company may appear. But even then some soft but important characteristics may be overlooked. That is why in most cases reports are added about organization charts, in-depth analysis of personnel and capabilities and all sorts of other soft data characteristics of a business.

As we are viewing websites as company assets we need to find a way in putting a price tag on them. In an ideal world our website should be incorporated in our financial report as an asset on the balance sheet. In some cases you will find websites on the balance sheet but then costs of designing are confused with asset value. A website is much more than the cost of designing and maintaining it. It is just like a brick and mortar shop where customers get in touch with our products and services and transactions are being made or leads generated. Reality is that I have never come across a company that is putting a realistic value of the website or ecommerce site within the books.

But is the performance of our website not included in our results?
This is a great question which I am sure of that many accountants love to ask. Isn't a company an entity where in the end everything may be deduced to a final figure, a

financial result? If our website or online shop adds to our sales and profits then you will see the results in the books. So what's the problem? In part this is true, in the end it must all lead to sales and profits. The problem is that if we want to assess the value of a website at a particular point in time not all results have materialized yet into financial results. We want to know what value is already present that will lead to financial results in the future.

A website is an engine of leads, sales and profits with still an amount of gas in its tanks. We want to know how much gas is available and how many miles it will take us. That is why we need to discover the strength or weaknesses of our website that will impact future results.

Why multiplying historic results will not do the trick

You might think that. Most business valuation methods will use a multiplier based upon historic financial results. The multiplier used is based upon the chosen method, market and specific situations. I am all in favor of using multipliers as we need to know the value that our website will bring us in the near future. But, and this is essential, a website is a special entity that has hidden strengths or weaknesses that will have an extra impact (positive or negative) on the financial results of the future. By only looking at the results up to this moment and multiplying these for future years you will either underestimate or overestimate the value of a website or online shop. That is the main reason why you need to take a deeper look into a website instead of only looking at the results up to now.

Using a financial valuation as a starting point

If financial results are available then it makes perfect sense to use these results in your valuation method. In the website valuation method I will explain further in this book I always start with a valuation based upon one or more economic or financial appraisal methods.

It all depends on the kind of website and the history of the available results how much weight this traditional financial approach may have in the total valuation. With an ecommerce website that is operating for many years a financial valuation will have a large impact on the total valuation. Sales and profits are transparent and readily available. Valuing an information-based website such as a general company website will offer extra challenges as it will be more difficult to attribute sales and profits to the website. With websites that only offer website content without any financial goal (like some blogs) we are not able to use a valuation method based upon financial results. Then only a qualitative method will suffice.

Then there are all sorts of mixed websites that do have a certain type of revenue model but are mainly concerned in building a loyal base of followers and readers. Many blogs and affiliates fall into this category using ads and affiliate banners as a form of monetization.

Whenever money is being made with a website I always start the valuation process with this hard data. There are many ways of valuing financial data, I prefer to use 2 or even more different approaches as each and every financial valuation method will have a different result. Best practice will be to average these differing results when using different methods or to choose one method that makes the most logical approach. The outcome will be my starting point for the qualitative valuation method.

Chapter 4: Components of a website valuation method

The website valuation method I introduce will be suitable for all sorts of websites but the type of website has an impact on how to utilize the different components of this method.

We already have made a distinction between information-based websites and online shops or ecommerce websites but there are many more variations. As a valuator of websites or an investor in websites you may come across all sorts of websites such as:

- Online shops or ecommerce websites
- Lead generating websites
- Blogs
- News websites
- Affiliate websites
- Job boards
- Online community websites
- Wiki websites
- Video or podcast websites

And the list goes on and on...

These different website types are aimed at serving specific needs within their markets. Some websites are aimed at driving direct sales such as ecommerce websites. Others are lead orientated such as many company- and B2B service-centered websites. Online communities are focused on getting followers and holding the attention of the community, in fact they are aimed at spending as much time on their platforms, in most cases serving ads as the core revenue model. Wiki websites are very much centered around sharing information, their direct monetizing model is difficult but they may be used as indirect lead generators. News websites make money form serving ads and adding paid subscribers.

Like I said before I wanted to come up with a website valuation method that is suitable for all sorts of websites whether a website does or does not generate sales and profits, whether it has a revenue model put in place or not and even when it loses money or does not generate any hard financial result whatsoever.

That will bring us to the central question of website valuation:

Which factors determine the value of a website?

That was the challenge I was given when I tried to establish a website valuation method. In my work as a digital marketing consultant I have come across hundreds of websites operating in all sorts of markets and making use of all types of websites and online shops. In 15 years of digital marketing I learned that there are a handful of key factors that determine the success of a website. Some of these factors are relatively easy to calculate, others are more difficult to work out, they are more intangible of nature. Before I had developed my website valuation method I was frequently asked to gauge the performance of a customer's website. I think I performed several hundreds of website checks as I called them before I even began to think of valuing a website. Through these website checks I was forced to think about performance indicators.

My conclusion was that most factors had a data-driven core but the conclusion was of a more qualitative nature. For instance, you could easily deduce the evolution of organic traffic from your Analytics report but you had to form a qualitative opinion about whether this evolution was good, bad or average. As I began developing my website valuation method I wondered if this qualitative side of valuing a website would not hinder objectivity. It took me a few days to come to the conclusion that every valuation method is either subjective or based upon extrapolations of historic data that may or may not materialize in the future. When a real estate appraiser is appraising your house it will need to assess the value of the condition of the interior and exterior of your house and the area it is located. When a business is valued many intangible factors like market authority and organizational capabilities are gauged. So we do not need an objective method of valuation, in fact striving for objectivity would be closing our eyes to reality. What we do need is a structured way of looking at the factors that create value in the same manner as we appraise real estate taking in all the value creating determinants.

So, set out to establish a website valuation method the first thing I had to do was to pinpoint the elements that created value for a website. I went through hundreds of Analytics reports of all sorts of websites, I analyzed all sorts of results my customers had made performing all sorts of actions and I benchmarked the results of one website to another trying to determine why one website performed better or worse than the other. Above all I was looking for characteristics that had a predictive strength for future value. In short I was looking for the drivers of website worth, the engines of a website that would propel it to better or worse results in years to come.

Eventually I came upon 5 key elements that create website value. The relative strength or weakness of these value drivers generate more or less value in the near future.

The 5 website value drivers
1. Organic traffic strength
2. Online authority strength
3. Technical strength
4. Advertising & social strength
5. Conversion strength

The above 5 elements have created value in the past and present but, and this is crucial, they also forecast value in the future. The great thing about these 5 elements is that you are able to see and gauge them right now. What is needed though is a qualitative rating of these elements and that requires a professional mindset. In this book I will give you guidelines that will help you determine a qualitative valuation for all these 5 elements.

And what about the financial results up to now?

The 5 website value drivers create value and value translates into results. By gauging the relative strength of these elements we will have a view on future results. That does not mean that we will have to close our eyes for past and present results of course. That is why I always use a financial valuation method (or several methods) to establish the worth of a website based upon financial results. Our website does produce results up to now (in most cases) and we need to calculate these results as a starting point.

Almost all financial valuation methods use a way of extrapolation of results for the future. This is important to notice. So there is already a format for future value based upon the **financial results** of our website. We will look at our 5 elements in order to extract the **extra hidden forces** of our website that will result in **extra financial gains or losses** that will be applied to the final result of our financial valuation.

The process of valuing a website

So, now we have the elements that create website value and we have financial data about sales and profits that can be used in a financial valuation method. The only question remains how to use all this in a structural way that finally leads to a price estimation of our website. My method is based upon a financial valuation using 1 or more existing financial valuation methods and 5 elements that discover the hidden forces that will add more or less value in the future. I tried several ways of combining all this in a good workable system and I have come upon the following method that is both logic, transparent and straightforward.

Part 1:   A financial valuation based upon financial data

Part 2:   A valuation based upon relative strength of the 5 key elements

In part 1 a financial valuation will lead to a value based upon hard financial results. In part 2 we will determine the relative strength of all 5 elements and calculate a weighed multiplier that will be applied to the value calculated in part 1.

So in part 2 we will add strengths and distract weaknesses that will finetune the value calculated in part 1. Sometimes the impact of the part 2 multiplier will have a significant impact on the final value, sometimes it will have a lower impact.

In general you could say that whenever hard financial data is more available the more weight the financial valuation will have whereas in situations when financial data is les available or less secure the qualitative valuation will have a greater impact. Establishing the value of an online shop or ecommerce site will lean much more on hard financial data than a company website that is generating leads or a blog that attracts large amounts of organic traffic but does not have a well-functioning monetizing system in place. So it all depends on what kind of website we are dealing with, but in general all websites may be valued according to this method.

Chapter 5: The 5 website value drivers

In chapter 4 we have introduced the 5 drivers of website value. Here we will explore these a bit further. In the next chapters they will come back when we start our valuation process.

Why do these 5 elements drive value?

Like I said before, I have gone through hundreds of websites analyzing what elements were responsible for the results these website were looking for. Although goals varied among different companies and websites it still boiled down to these 5 elements. Here I will get into each different element explaining why it attributes to the worth of a website and why it will have an impact on future results. It is this impact on future results that is the important part of these elements.

Website Value Driver 1: Organic traffic strength

Organic traffic is free and relevant. Those two qualifications are extremely important in today's competitive online environment. Whatever your website objectives are, you need relevant visitors in order to meet your goals. Why is organic traffic almost always very relevant to your website and goals? Because it is mainly your website content that drives it. In most cases your website content tells much about your market, products and services so you will be attracting people with an interest in your market. In other cases you use your website content to attract visitors for goals like clicking on ads or affiliate banners. When doing your job proper your website content or target audience aligns with your advertisements. So in most cases organic traffic is by definition relevant traffic.

Another way of looking at relevance is to analyze conversions per traffic channel. In approximately 70% of all the many websites I analyzed organic traffic is the number 1 ranking channel on conversion rate. I must add that this included branded keywords (search queries on the name of the company or brand) but even without branded keywords this channel was the best performing on conversion rates.

And what about the fact that this traffic is free of charge? Well, that is unbelievably important in a world where the cost of online advertising is rising through the roof. I must add that driving organic traffic to a website does not come without efforts or costs. It takes lots of time, energy and money to attract organic traffic. Think of writing website content, hiring SEO specialists, sharing your content and building an online community that will come back for more.

But why is a strong performance on organic traffic a value driver for the future? Because organic traffic is like an engine, when the organic engine shifts in gear it will not stop easily. It will continue to rise or even shift to a higher gear. A strong performance in organic traffic will tell you much about the health of a website. In the next chapters I will explain when we can talk about organic traffic strength or weakness.

Website Value Driver 2: Online authority strength

There are several degrees of online authority. You can have a weak, average or strong online authority. But what is it? There are several definitions going around on the web but in essence online authority applies to being a thought leader on a specific subject or market that is propagated through an online presence. The result of being an online authority is that people regard you as being credible and legitimate about your market or specialization.

How does a strong online authority play to your advantage? In several ways. People may go to your website for additional information about your market or products because they value your meaning. Other websites may link to your website as they refer to your website for further details about a certain topic. Your social media accounts may be followed closely as people value the news you spread. Even so important, organic authority will lead in most cases to higher rankings on important keywords within your market as search engines also endorse your website content as authentic and relevant.

In fact becoming an online authority within a specific market you are specialized in should be high on your list of online objectives as it is very rewarding. It is not easily obtained of course and has much to do with building a positive reputation. Like Warren Buffet said: "It takes 20 years to build a reputation and five minutes to ruin it."

When you are perceived as an online authority in your market it will propel this authority into the future (if not abused of course). So a website with online authority will benefit from that authority for years to come. Of course taking care of that authority and living up to expectations comes with the territory of being a thought leader.

Website Value Driver 3: Technical Strength

With technical strength we are referring to the technical status of a website. This may be interpreted broadly. The central question here is if the website lives up to the current standards. You may think of accessibility of the website to all sorts of devices, swift loading times, a customer-friendly navigation, properly installed statistical packages that capture online behavior, leads and sales management and a content management system that allows all designated employees to build and alternate website content. Of course the list may go on and on but I always focus on the most important technical issues that are relevant for the moment I am performing the valuation. Technical demands and issues may change over time.

As with all other website value drivers this element also has its impact on future results. A website that is in a proper and sound technical shape will not lose its shape overnight. It also has a cost-saving side as large technical updates or a complete makeover won't be necessary in the near future.

Website Value Driver 4: Advertising & social strength

Driving traffic to a website is a challenge. We already talked about organic traffic and the efforts of SEO but there are other channels that drive traffic. Social media and (online) advertising are the main sources of relevant traffic but it may come at relatively high costs. Social media channels like Facebook, Instagram, Twitter, Pinterest and YouTube may drive large amounts of traffic at relatively low costs if managed well. I must confess that in today's online world it becomes more and more difficult to attract new traffic through social media. Timelines have changed overtime and the viewability of company's posts is getting a real challenge prompting many companies to either abandon these channels as traffic drivers or advertise on them. YouTube is an important channel to build awareness and may be great of driving traffic that is in search of information but it may also be used as an advertising medium.

That brings us to the next challenge, online advertising. Of course Google Ads and Bing Ads pop to mind but there are numerous other online advertising opportunities that can be used to drive relevant traffic. I will focus my attention on online advertising as offline advertising may be helpful as well but as it is extremely difficult to measure we cannot properly measure its results.

A well-managed social media and online advertising strategy will bring online results that exceed the cost of time, energy and advertising costs. As an experienced digital marketing consultant I know the difficulty of arriving at such a situation. But when you are able to make a positive return on your social and advertising efforts you not only have created a money maker but you also have learned the lessons of making paid traffic profitable. And that, my friends, is worth even more for future gains. It is also precisely the reason why I have put this here as a website value driver.

In analyzing websites and results I found that when a well-managed advertising and/or social media strategy is being implemented it not only drives online results in the here and now but it will keep on driving results. What is the underlying reason for this phenomenon? In my opinion it has everything to do with the learning and experience curve effect. Running an effective online advertising campaign takes time and experience.

As most digital advertising specialists know, it takes time and know-how to optimize online campaigns and this is true for all advertising platforms whether it be Google Ads, Bing Ads, Facebook, Youtube, LinkedIn or any other platform. The good thing about all this learning by making mistakes is that finally you will come to a point that you know what works and your campaign settings will be almost perfect in order to obtain your goals. From that point on only minor optimizations will suffice to drive in results. That is why a well-run social media or online advertising campaign will add value in the future whereas a badly run campaign will lose time and money now and in the future.

Website Value Driver 5: Conversion strength

Having a website that converts into your objectives and goals sounds great. But there is more to it than meets the eye. A website with relatively much direct traffic and returning visitors will convert better than a website that is constantly attracting new visitors. That doesn't mean that the latter one is worse at converting. Another thing to bear in mind is the difference between goals and objectives. A website goal is the ultimate thing you want to accomplish, for instance a concrete lead or a sale in your ecommerce website. Objectives will be the smaller steps towards your goal such as newsletter subscriptions, downloads of white papers, followers on LinkedIn or whatever. So in many cases there are more conversions to watch for and objectives are easier to achieve than goals.

What is important for us with respect to the value of a website? What we ultimately want to see is a website that entices people to take the actions we want them to take. We can calculate conversion rates for all objectives and goals and we can compare these rates between traffic channels. You could say that a good converting website is one that is outperforming the market. The difficulty is that in most cases we do not know what average conversion rates are in each and every market.

What I can say is that a conversion rate for an online shop over 2% is good but here too are many differences in markets and websites. So what are we looking for? In general I want to see conversions among all traffic channels with lower conversion rates for new visitors and better rates for returning visitors or existing customers. I am particularly interested in conversions of new organic traffic and even more in conversions from traffic originating from online advertising or social media channels as these channels offer the biggest challenge. The difference between new and returning visitors is not always easy to make as many people remove cookies or they use a VPN network. Traffic coming from online advertising or social media is for a large part new and examining. If a website can turn these visitors in (potential) customers, followers or subscribers in a rather substantial and structural way than you might say that this website converts well. But I must confess, gauging the conversion strength of a website is not an easy task and it takes some analyzing and sound thinking and pondering to come up with a verdict about this strength.

I always start looking at conversion rates and comparisons between traffic channels. I also try to obtain bench marking figures. In my practice I can compare hundreds of data of different websites and ecommerce sites which make it a bit easier but it still is a challenge to measure conversion strength just looking at analytical data.

Another approach I use is going through the website just as a real estate appraiser will walk through your house and garden. If you have two gardens with similar data (same square meters, same orientation to the sun and maybe even the same amount of trees) there still may be huge differences between the value of one garden to the other. It's the same with conversion strength.

I always use the AIDA model to look for conversion strength. The AIDA model (Attention, Interest, Desire, Action) describes the steps that lead to conversion. What a good converting website must do is leading the visitor through the last 3 steps in a customer friendly and logical way. The attention phase is normally behind us when entering a website. But raising interest, inciting desire and evoking action is something one website excels over another. A good converting website takes care of the 3 steps towards action. By going through a website you can notice them too.

Making a website that converts well is not a simple task. It takes a lot of time and energy to arrive to a situation that goals and objectives are met by traffic originating from all kinds of sources.

Just as with the other 4 website value drivers a good conversion strength will keep on offering value. The blood, sweat and tears you put into the conversion optimization process will not evaporate overnight, it will keep on delivering results.

Chapter 6: Weighing the 5 website value drivers

Before we will get into the website valuation process I need to explain how I found out why the 5 website value drivers will add value in the future and how important each element is in driving that value.

As I said before I have analyzed hundreds of websites trying to detect what elements really matter for future results. How did I do that?

Explaining cause and effect through analyzing data

I started out with a few websites, ecommerce websites and information-based websites, trying to find what elements were responsible for online results. In the beginning I focused on 2 online goals: lead generation for information- based websites and sales for online shops. I went through Analytics data trying to find where the results originated from. I also went through changes these websites had undergone, optimizations in search engine marketing and online advertising, social media strategies and implementations, new content building, new website designs, technical optimizations and conversion optimizations. Although not all optimizations materialized in better results most of them did.

But I was looking for more than only direct results. I wanted to know whether an improvement in conversions would last and how long it would last after a particular optimization.

Finally I came up with these 4 elements:

1. Organic traffic strength
2. Online advertising and social media strength
3. Conversion strength
4. Technical strength

Judging each and every website on these 4 elements became easier as I was analyzing more and more data from more and different websites. I began to develop an eye for strengths on these 4 elements. I also added more soft objectives such as newsletter subscriptions and I found out that still these 4 elements were key contributors to these objectives.

Still I had a few websites before me that did not have any particular strength in one of these four elements. Organic traffic was growing nicely but they did not follow any structural SEO strategy although they did share news about their products and markets, they did not advertise online and were not active on social media. The technical side of these websites was okay but conversion wasn't on their minds. Still they drove in organic traffic and lots of direct traffic and recurring visitors. These visitors also converted into (most softer) goals.

I could attribute the relative success of these websites to organic traffic strength but I felt that wasn't right. What caused the relative success of these websites? They all had one thing in common, they were relatively well-known brands within their markets with a long company history and plenty of existing customers. They were authorities in their fields and this authority filtered through to an online authority. The success of their historical efforts in building and growing a company overflowed to their online success. That is how I discovered website value driver number 5: Online authority strength.

Comparing the strength of our 5 website value drivers

Not all website value drivers are equally important in adding value to a website. Mind, I was not looking for value drivers that contributed to past results, I was looking for elements that were generating results in the future. Some elements drove value for a long time to come, others added value for a shorter period of time. Then there was the impact itself, some had a bigger impact than others.

In analyzing data from different websites I found that there was a regularity in the future value these 5 elements added, although there were differences between some types of website. I also looked at the intensity and duration of the impact for each website value driver.

This is what I found:

Website Value Driver:	Position impact intensity	Position impact duration
Organic strength	1	2
Online authority strength	3	1
Technical strength	5	4
Advertising & social media strength	2	5
Conversion strength	4	3

Organic strength had the biggest impact on future value and the impact duration was relatively long. Free and relevant organic traffic that is growing adds significant value to the website in the future. The duration of this growth is relatively long but of course it is depended upon following through the strategy that has led to this growth.

The impact duration on future value from online authority strength was the longest (far out) and it added considerable future value but not as much as organic strength did. Organic strength implies that more and more new and relevant traffic will find its way to a website whereas online authority strength is funded more on recurrent traffic.

Technical strength does not have a huge impact on future value, the same goes for its duration. If you have a brilliantly designed website using the newest techniques you may have a head start on your competitors but not for long as they too will eventually use the same techniques.

Running an almost perfectly optimized online advertising campaign (it will never be 100% perfect) and a social media strategy that has a larger output than input is extremely important for driving future value. It comes in second after organic strength. The duration of the impact coming from a well-managed online advertising and/or social media campaign may be short. You will need to optimize further as advertising and social media platforms are constantly adding and changing settings and competitors may out-bid or out-perform you. You might say it's the same with organic strength, but that is not what I found. Even if you have built your organic traffic through a wise SEO strategy and you would stop that from one moment to the other I found that organic traffic still grows on for 2 to 3 years (in general). The same can't be said of a well running online advertising campaign.

And what about conversion strength? You would expect that a good converting website offers much future value. Well, it does, but I found out that the impact on results was bigger from driving extra traffic (as from organic + advertising / social media strength) and that the impact on conversions coming from the security of an online authority cannot be surpassed by a stream-lined conversion process. However, a well-established and optimized conversion process does have a long impact, it will not stop converting overnight.

Combining intensity and duration of impact

There is also a difference between the amount of intensity and length of duration each website value driver has. The intensity of the impact of organic strength and advertising & social media strength was much greater than that of the number 3 to

5. The same goes for the duration impact where online authority was outshining the other 4 elements.

The graph below puts everything into perspective:

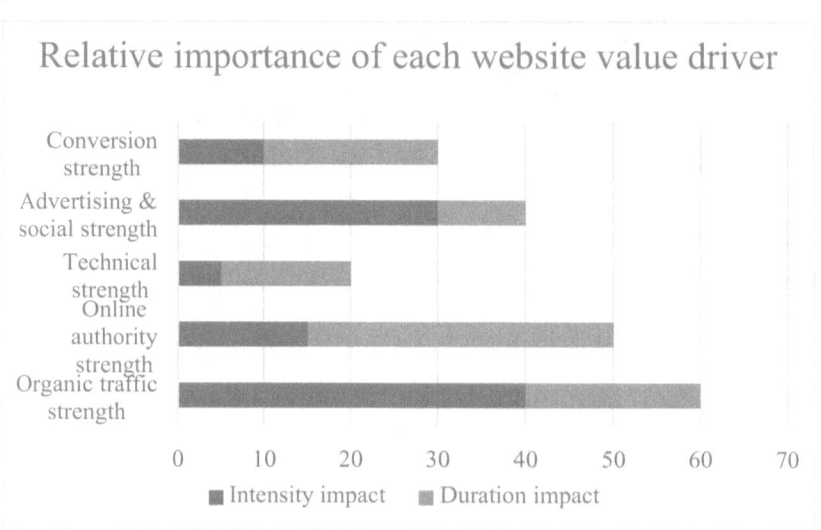

When we combine both impacts of each website value driver we will see that organic traffic strength has the biggest overall impact on future value of our website followed by online authority and advertising & social media strength. Conversion strength and technical strength do not have a large intensity impact on future value but their duration impact is relatively strong making them number 4 and 5 on our impact list.

Calculating the weighting factor of each website value driver

Now that we have a combined impact on duration and intensity of each website value driver we can calculate the combined weighting factor. Before we will establish weighting factors I have to add that the impacts I found could be different among certain websites or types of websites. The above mentioned impacts are an aggregate of all websites. But I also found that the differences were relatively minor.

In general I use the following weighting factors:

Website Value Driver:	Position combined impact	Weighting factor
Organic strength	1	30%
Online authority strength	2	25%
Advertising & social media strength	3	20%
Conversion strength	4	15%
Technical strength	5	10%

When applying weighting factors in valuing an individual website I may calculate with different weighting factors between the 5 value drivers. Some websites are very strong or weak in 1 specific field that will have an important impact on future value.

Let's say you come across a website that is internationally focused and has a great online advertising campaign running in all parts of the world. Organic traffic may be very feeble compared to the traffic originating from this online advertising campaign. This is not uncommon as it is hard to attract organic traffic across different global regions. But when the advertising campaign has a splendid ROI and a proven track record of high conversion rates than I would weigh this element more heavily.

If a website is still performing well but it is technically outdated I would also give more weight to this factor as it will have a larger than average impact on future results.

Chapter 7: The website valuation process

Now that we have explored the 5 website value drivers it is time to look at the complete process of website valuation. Up to now we have talked much about these 5 website value drivers but that is not where we start our valuation process. We begin with nothing less than a good-old-fashioned financial valuation based upon hard financial data.

Step 1: Financial valuation

In this phase of the valuation process we will look at historical data which we extrapolate to the future in order to get a financial value of the website at this moment of time. There are several financial valuation methods that I will discuss in the next chapter.

In general, all financial valuation methods focus on hard financial historical data. Sales, earnings, cash flows, EBIT, EBITDA or assets are the main multiples here. Most financial valuation methods multiply the result for 3 to 5 years or they look at historical data from the last 3 to 5 years as a benchmark for the current value. Sometimes multipliers go further up to 7 or 9 years. It all depends on the choice of method and mutual agreement of the parties involved.

I always prefer to let this part of the valuation being executed by an objective accountant.

The real challenge in this phase is to attribute all these data to your website. With an eommerce website this is not a very difficult task to perform but when dealing with an information-based website that drives in leads for the sales department it is another cup of tea. There are several ways in attributing sales to websites, there are hard sales and profits that may be directly attributed to the website but there are also supporting attributions that have played a part in the company results. When operating a sound and solid CRM system or an administration system that keeps track of attributing sales per channel this would be very helpful.

The result of this financial valuation is a fixed amount in Dollars or Euro's or whatever currency you are calculating in.

Step 2: Deciding on the weighting factors of the 5 website value drivers

When the financial valuation is finished we will continue with our more qualitative valuation based upon the 5 website value drivers. We will have to keep in mind that within the financial valuation phase hard results are also extrapolated with future results in mind so here we need to focus on the extra future value these 5 elements will drive to our website. But first we will have to add weighting factors to our 5 elements.

In the previous chapter I introduced general weighting factors that on average gave a realistic view for each single website value driver. Here we will have to decide whether these general weighting factors would be applicable on this particular website or not.

When could weighting factors deviate from the average aggregated factors?

- **When one single website value driver is significantly more important than you would expect**
  This could be the case for a high growth website that is heavily depended upon online advertising as its engine of growth or a website that is technically completely out-of-date.

- **When the website operates in a specific market that makes one website value driver more important than the other**
  For instance when a website operates in a market where online advertising opportunities are barred by important platforms such as gambling, smoking, medicines. In these cases organic strength may be much more important than advertising and social media strength.

- **A number of other specific situations**
  There are numerous specific situations that may call for adjustments in the general weighting factors. When you are dealing with a relatively new website some value drivers are not easy to gauge which may be a cause for adjusting weighting factors. It may also occur that someone is interesting in buying a specific website because of the organic traffic it creates. Then other drivers are less important as the buyer is mainly focused at its organic traffic strength. There are other situations that need a different than average weighing so you really have to think things through before picking your weighting factors.

Step 3: Assessing the relative strength of each website value driver

Here the true process of website valuation starts. Each and every website value driver must be estimated and valued. The best thing to do is to make a strength and weaknesses report about each element. Fortunately in most cases there is hard data that you can work with. Analytics reports and CRM systems are very helpful in making this strengths / weaknesses analysis. But you will also need a specialist who is able to see through all these data.

Remember, this part of the website valuation process is called qualitative valuation. Hard data will help you arrive to your conclusions but in the end a label must be attached to each website value driver and that should be an informed and substantiated label, good or bad.

Like with all other valuations and estimations, you are not allowed to stop thinking and let the data take over the process. The reason is simple, there are too many ways of valuing so data alone will not be the decisive element.

Step 4: Adding a multiplier to each website value driver

After assessing the relative strength or weakness of a single website value driver you will have to put a "price label" on it. Well, you might do that, but I prefer to work with multipliers. This, my friends, is the core of our valuation process. By translating the strength of a website value driver into a single multiplier you are in essence pricing that website value driver.

How to use multipliers? I will come back to this all important process later in this book but in general it works like this:

A multiplier of 1 is neutral, which means there is no **extra future** value expected on top of the extrapolation of historical data derived from the financial valuation.

Again, this is very important to keep in mind: we are looking for extra future value or extra future lower value for each website value driver with regard to the financial value already calculated. A multiplier of 1 does not have any extra impact (good or bad) on the figure that was the result of the financial valuation. So, in fact, when you are gauging the strength of an important website value driver (like organic traffic strength) with a high weighting factor and your multiplier is 1 it will not affect the value derived from your financial valuation.

When you decide to put a multiplier above 1 it will add extra value to the worth derived from the financial valuation. Of course a multiplier below 1 will extract value from that worth.

In practice I will use multipliers varying from 0 to 2. That implies that a single website value driver may at its maximum have an impact of 2 times the worth calculated from the financial valuation (adjusted by its weighting factor of course) and at its minimum it will erase the financial valuation worth. Talking in absolute figures this will balance out (double the amount or subtracting that amount to zero). In practice we will not see such big movements as we are dealing with 5 website value drivers all adjusted by their weighting factors.

Another very important notion is that the more hard financial data is available the lesser the impact of multipliers should be. So when you are dealing with valuing an online shop where almost all financial data is available over a substantial period of time you should apply narrower bandwidths of multipliers. In practice I will use a maximum of 1,5 and a minimum of 0,5 with E-commerce websites.

We will come back at applying multipliers when we are going to some examples of website valuations.

Step 5: Calculating the final worth of a website

So, what do we have up to now? We have a financial worth of our website, we added weighting factors to each individual website value driver and we applied multipliers to them. Now we can put all elements of our website valuation process together and arrive to a final worth of our website.

Putting it all into 1 scheme it will look like this:

Financial valuation
Using 1 or several financial valuing methods

Qualitative valuation
5 website value drivers | Weighting factors | Assigning multipliers

Final website worth calculation
Adding all weighed multipliers | Arriving at 1 single multiplier

Chapter 8: Financial valuation methods and challenges

In the previous chapter we have discussed the 5 steps of the website valuation process. Before performing a complete website valuation I want to expand on that first important step, the financial valuation phase.
As the financial valuation will be the base of our website valuation method we need to understand what methods are available and how we can use them to come up with the right starting point of the further steps.

First and foremost we need hard financial data to perform a thorough financial valuation. Here the first problems will arise, especially with information based websites or lead generating websites.

Attribution of sales, profits and costs
Which sales and profits may be contributed to our website? That is the number 1 challenge in our financial valuation phase. Of course there are many differences between websites and markets. An obvious difference is one between information based websites and ecommerce websites.

Attribution challenges for ecommerce websites
An online shop will not cause much problems in attribution. We can attribute sales and gross margins to our website. But here the attribution of costs may be a challenge. Not when we are a 100% pure ecommerce company handling one single online shop. It will be a bit trickier when we are operating a bunch of ecommerce websites if we want to value each different one on its own merits. The biggest problem arises when we operate an ecommerce website alongside a physical shop or a mixture of a B2B company with personal sales and an ecommerce website. What costs may be directly attributed

to our online shop and what to other commercial activities that will lead to results?

We may look for answers in our CRM systems and order processing administration. In many cases sales have to be attributed to one specific channel. Cost attribution is much more difficult although there are many ways of establishing a good model of attribution spreading fixed and variable costs among channels.

Another challenge may be the amount of historical data our online shop can provide. If we are running a steady and stable online shop for many years our figures will be well-balanced. But I have come across many ecommerce websites with relatively short lifetime spans and very fluctuating or fast growing results that makes a financial valuation more difficult.

In most cases however, we can come up with enough usable data that we are able to perform a sound and solid financial valuation of our ecommerce website.

Attribution challenges for non-ecommerce websites

Attribution for websites that do not drive direct online sales come in all sorts of shapes and types. Think of news websites and blogs that mainly earn money through renting space for advertisers or company websites that are aimed at generating leads for their sales departments. But there are lots and lots of more specific websites that do not sell stuff directly to customers. Job boards, social media platforms, business directories, auction websites, affiliate websites, online communities. There are a myriad of websites that do have some sort of a monetizing system but do not sell directly and there are even numerous websites with sometimes a considerable amount of traffic that do not have any monetizing method nor objective. We will discuss this particular website market further in this book. But even when there is a solid sales or profit goal with a non-ecommerce website attribution of sales and profits may be a cause of some headaches.

What are the main challenges?

- **Attributing sales and profits to each channel**
  Who made the sale, the website that made first contact with the customer or our sales team that added advice and signed the contract?

- **Determining where the customer journey started**
  In today's online world a large part of new business comes from an online query. But not all. Word of mouth and physical networking are still strong lead generators. Off line starters may be hard to recognize as hardly any footprints will be left.

- **Administering the touchpoints of a customer journey**
  We can decide to use a shared attribution model. Let's say 40% for the initial contact, 30% for follow-up advice and 30% for closing the deal. But will all these touchpoints be visible to us? And what about a customer who at one time asks a question to our sales team and the other time will look something up within our website?

- **Backtracking sales and profits**
  Although we may be trying to attribute sales to channels we will almost inevitably lose attributions in the process. Some sales will be made in our shop or by telephone without being able to detect which touchpoints have been made. Backtracking these sales will be hard or highly questionable at least.

So how to use hard data in our financial valuation?

It all depends on the availability of financial data in order to perform a solid financial valuation. In most ecommerce environments there will be enough hard data available to make this valuation. In other situations we will have to use what is there. We may sift through our order processing or CRM systems and we can use data from our sales department as well as from online statistics such as Analytics to discern online and off line leads. We can also use a lead to order ratio (the percentage of leads that will materialize in orders) and backtrack the customer journey. Most of all we will have to use our common sense and make a practical and workable way of translating hard data to channels trying to discover the added value of our website to these financial data.

The impact of less qualitative financial data on the valuation process

A question arises when you understand that there is a difference between a situation where hard financial data for a website is readily available and when that is not the case. Should we give more weight to the financial valuation phase when more hard data for our website is available, and consequently less weight when this data is less qualitative of nature? Yes, we should. This makes sense. The more we can deduce value from hard and solid financial data the better we can extrapolate these data to future value. But we must keep in mind that the 5 website value drivers also add extra (or less) value regardless of the availability of historical data. That being said, we must use as much hard financial data as possible and the discrepancy between websites with more and less attributable data must affect our website valuation process.

How do I go about adjusting the weight of the financial valuation process?

Like I said before we must give more weight to the financial valuation phase when dealing with a direct result driven website (such as an ecommerce site). However, I will not adjust this weighing in the resulting worth based upon the financial valuation. I will adjust it in the qualitative website valuation phase. When dealing with for instance an ecommerce website with a relatively long historical track record offering much financial data I will maximize the multipliers for each of the 5 website value drivers to 1,5 and minimize it to 0,5.

When dealing with a website that cannot offer solid attributable financial data the multiplier of our 5 value drivers is wider with a minimum of 0 and a maximum of 2. That is if and when some hard financial data is available in the first place. There are situations when no financial attributable data exists. This may be the case for websites that do not drive sales, leads or sell advertising space. Some websites only offer information. That does not mean that these websites have no worth, absolutely not, but we cannot use a financial valuation method as our base of a qualitative valuation adjusting it with a multiplier.

So the bandwidth of our multiplier is relatively narrow when we are dealing with a website that offers a solid track record of hard financial data, it is much wider when data is questionable or difficult to attribute. Finally, when no financial data is available we must abandon step 1, the financial valuation process and go right to step 2. We will adjust our method in such a situation, not working with multipliers but with Dollar amounts (or whatever currency you are using). I will discuss this situation further in the book.

Now let's have a look at some financial valuation methods.

A large choice of financial valuation methods

In valuing an asset you can choose your pick among several methods of financial valuation and an almost endless list of rules of thumb. Here we will discuss the most important ones and I will also add some pros and cons regarding the valuation of a website.

Before we start I want to emphasize that we will use the value that is derived from a financial valuation in the further process of website valuation. So the outcome of this first step in the website valuation process is very important. That being said, we also have to acknowledge that this outcome will vary among each and every method you will use. You could say that this will diminish its value for our objective, trying to come up with the best estimated value for a website. This is all true, but the business of valuation will always be one of estimations and best possible practices. The end result may be presented as one single amount in Dollars or Euro's but this price label consists of many assumptions and extrapolations.

Here I will discuss the most important financial valuation methods commonly used in valuing assets and businesses. I will give a brief explanation of each method, its pros and cons and its usefulness for valuing a website.

The following financial valuation methods will be discussed:

A] Income based methods

1. Discounted Cash Flow method
2. Capitalization of Earnings method

B] Asset based methods

C] Market based methods

D] Rules of thumb

A] Income based methods

In valuing an asset or business looking at the free stream of money coming in makes sense. With an income based valuation method we do not focus our attention on the asset itself but on its capacity to earn money. Most income based methods are cash flow orientated as this gives a more objective view of income than profits (profits may be more easily manipulated).

By far the most popular income based valuation method is the Discounted Cash Flow method. The other one is the Capitalization of Earnings method. The difference between these 2 methods lies in its flexibility. The DCF method is more flexible in taking in fluctuating streams of cash flow and different growth rates. Here we will discuss both of them.

1. Discounted Cash Flow method

The Discounted Cash Flow method is a valuation method that is using historical financial data as a basis for future earnings. The essence of this method is calculating the amount of money an asset will make in the near future. In order to come up with that figure we will need to know the cash we will earn in the coming years and the cash it will take to run our business or website. The difference is the free cash flow. We will also have to adjust these future earnings with the risks involved. 1 million Dollars now has more value to us than an expected 1 million Dollars in 5 years. So we need to adjust the future cash flow for the time value of money. That part is the discount factor of this method.

What is needed to calculate a value based upon the Discounted Cash Flow method?

Well, we need a bunch of good and solid financial data. We need to know what cash our website or ecommerce website will generate in the future, that is incoming cash and outgoing cash. We can make an assessment about that upon our historical data. That is a bit risky of course as the world of yesterday will not be the world of tomorrow, certainly in our field of constant changing online challenges. Another option would be a business plan that takes into account some future challenges, but again it is only a plan however solid it is made.

When all future free cash flows are charted we will need to know what kind of return on our investment we will need. We will also need to know what the cost of attracting debt will be. We then can calculate the Weighted Average Cost of Capital or WACC. This is a needed exercise to calculate the discount of future cash flows. Calculating the cost of debt will not be the hardest part as interest rates of bank loans are widely available. The biggest challenge will be what kind of return on our investment we will need. That is a tough one as risk will enter the equation. Risk determines returns. If obtaining the calculated future cash flows is surrounded with substantial risk we will need to have a higher return. But what will be the risk we are running?

This is not the place to delve further into this rather complicated way of calculating the value of an asset. There are many online and off line sources that you can use to really understand the ins and outs of the DCF method. In theory it is maybe the best method available, in practice it is surrounded by many uncertainties and relies heavily on assumptions of future results.

Advantages of the DCF method:

1. The DCF method is taking a look at the future through existing or calculated future cash flows. You could say that this method is the most future bound valuation method.

2. Although it is not an easy task to fulfill, by calculating a value based upon the DCF method you will need to focus on financial data and future values. This will give a good insight into your website (or the one you are willing to invest in).

3. The DCF method is focused on cash flows, not on profits that are always more malleable.

Disadvantages of the DCF method:

1. If the data you use to calculate free cash flows is not correct the outcome will be very questionable. The same goes for the risk perception in calculating the WACC. The DCF method is a calculation method that needs hard data but these data are not fixed and hard.

2. In many situations there is no cash flow data available for websites. Either there is a lack of hard financial historical data or it is too hard to estimate future cash flows in this ever changing online world.

3. The DCF method appears to take into account future value but it is solely focused on cash flow without looking at the underlying forces that will drive cash flow.

Usefulness of the DCF method

If enough financial data is available and the assumptions about future cash flows are sound and logic I would certainly use the DCF method for the financial valuation phase. It is particularly helpful in the valuation of ecommerce websites.

2. Capitalization of Earnings method

The Capitalization of Earnings method is either profit or cash flow orientated. As profits are always a bit questionable many prefer a cash flow orientated approach. How does it work? It starts with computing the expected cash flow for a specified period. The second step is to divide this cash flow estimate by the capitalization rate. The capitalization rate represents the risk an investor is willing to take translated into a return on investment. This rate may vary depending among the website or business involved.

There are large similarities between the DCF method and CoE method as they will look at current and historical earnings or cash flows to try to establish future cash flows. With the CoE method the historical growth rate of cash flow will be extrapolated to the future. In essence this does not allow for fluctuations in future cash flows. In that respect the Capitalization of Earnings method is more simple of use than the Discounted Cash Flow method.

Advantages of the CoE method for website valuations:

1. It is a straightforward method in trying to calculate future earnings based upon the annual growth rate of the income a website has generated in the past.

2. It does take into account that future cash flows are important for the generation of value.

3. When valuing a website with a stable historical cash flow operating in a stable environment this method is a great one to use. This may be the case for online market leaders within specific market niches.

Disadvantages of the CoE method:

1. For many websites the CoE method is too rigid. The online environment is evolving in such a rapid pace and new competitors may lure behind every fine looking tree that an emphasis on historical growth is not always the best solution.

2. Just like with the DCF method it does not look into the engines of growth. Particularly with the CoE method this may cause problems as earnings up to now may be rosy but the engines may be running out of fuel.

3. This method also needs abundant hard financial data to calculate with.

B] Asset based methods

In essence there are 2 assets based valuation methods used in valuing a business. The first is a simple one that looks at the balance sheet of a company. The assets will be added and its liabilities are deducted. This going concern approach may be simple but it is also not representing the true value of its assets. Most assets on a balance sheet are calculated upon their original acquisition cost but that does not represent fair market value. That is why the second asset based method is more appropriate. It concentrates on the Net Asset Value of the company's assets, that is the fair market value of all assets minus the amount of liabilities.

Calculating the Net Asset Value

The main objective is trying to add all assets that make up the value of a company and adjust all prices to fair market value, that is the present value of an asset. The challenge will be to establish common grounds for determining the market value for each and every asset bought maybe many years ago.

But there is still another larger challenge. When looking at a company's balance sheet you will detect some assets such as real estate, machinery or vehicles but in general there is much more value within a company than the assets stated in the balance sheet. What about the company's know-how or market formula that has been optimized during several years? Maybe a company is using a specific procedure to come up with a better product or a lower price than competitors. These are all assets that are not included in the balance sheet. Of course you may put a price tag on them but without a valuation method gauging these assets this will be questionable. What about liabilities? Here things are much simpler. Most liabilities are in fair market value, so the only major concern are the assets themselves.

What about its usefulness for website valuation?

Asset based valuation methods are used to asses complete businesses. Instead of looking at future incomes, an asset based model is concentrated on the assets themselves. In essence this is a good approach but it does not help us at valuing our website. To say it in another way: website valuation should be part of the asset based valuation method but it does not supply answers in how to establish the worth of a website. The same goes for coming up with the fair market value of real estate that is included in the balance sheet. We still need the expertise of a real estate appraiser to gauge the current value of it.

So, in the total valuation of a company the asset based method is a sound and logic way of obtaining the current value of its operation but it relies heavily upon valuing its important hard and soft assets.

Advantages of the Asset Based method:

1. It takes into account that the value of a company is based upon the net value of all its assets. As a general approach this makes a lot of sense.

2. It leaves room for assets that are not included in the balance sheet or are not valued at fair market prices.

Disadvantages of the Asset Based method:

1. It will not give exact guidelines in how to value hard or soft assets (such as formulas or brands) at fair market value. It often generates more questions than answers.

2. With an asset based mindset you may overlook underlying forces that will drive future growth or decline.

C] Market based methods

Market based valuation methods are primarily focused on market transactions of similar assets, companies or websites. The central question here is what the selling price was for recent transactions of other companies or assets that are operating within the same or comparable market. In our world of websites and ecommerce sites one would look for similar websites that have been sold recently.

Applying a market based valuation method it will be the selling price of other websites that becomes our benchmark for valuation. Is this a valid method? Yes, it may be a valid method if conditions are similar and there are enough transactions made. If there is enough data available one could apply this method. The stock market more or less uses a market based approach. Of course when you are buying a share on one of the world's stock exchanges you are buying exactly the same share as someone else. But even with Initial Public Offerings (new stocks coming on the market) one uses a market based method upon deciding what the initial stock price should be. They will be looking at IPO's of similar companies to establish their share price, but of course other methods will also be used as no single company is exactly similar to another one.

In real estate markets this method also is useful in determining prices of similar real estate sold within the same neighborhood, although this will not suffice in valuing each single house within the same street.

The practice of using a market based valuation method looks easy on the surface. You may search for websites that are comparable to that of yours, try to find out what the selling price was and take an average. By doing that you should be fine. Will you? I do not think so. First and foremost, it will be difficult to find recent transactions of really similar websites. By looking at a website you will not see the data behind it. Adding to that is that really similar websites do not exist. The same goes for the results they are making. With public companies one can search through a bundle of financial reports in order to gauge their strength. With websites and ecommerce sites you will not be able to see the facts and figures even when the website is part of a public company. There are major drawbacks in using this method for valuing a website. Still it may be used to set some picket poles or establishing a bandwidth, but even then one has to be extremely careful.

Advantages of the Market Based method:

1. Useful in determining a roughly based bottom and top price for a website.

2. Very good exercise in getting a grasp on selling prices within a similar market.

Disadvantages of the Market Based method:

1. In non-public environments there is insufficient data available to gauge the selling price of an asset.

2. Particularly with websites you will not be looking at the internal strength of a website. You will not learn about the future value of a particular website by looking at the selling price of another website.

3. There are no 2 websites the same. They may operate within the same market but that does not mean that they perform on the same level. There are so much variables that may be different, not only financial KPI's but also concerning the 5 website value drivers.

D] Rules of Thumb

Especially in valuing small or middle large companies a myriad of rules of thumb valuation methods are being used. These rules of thumbs may also be useful in valuing the financial part of a website valuation.

In essence these rules of thumb are a derivative of the market based valuation approach as they use on average rules for similar markets.

What kind of rules of thumb methods are in use?

There are many available. You may come across the following rules of thumb:

- **2 to 5 times net profit**
- **0,75 to 1,5 times gross revenue**

- **2 to 5 times discretionary cash flow**
- **2 to 4 times EBITDA**
- **3 to 5 times EBIT**

And there are more. What I personally like about these rules of thumb is that it focuses all attention on 1 single figure that is relatively easy to calculate and mix it with a market based multiplier. Of course, using any kind of rule of thumb will not give you the exact value but neither will any other valuation method. But there are major drawbacks too. What figure should you focus on, cash flow, profit, EBIT? With every choice of parameter another outcome will present itself. That doesn't look reassuring.

And what multiplier to use? In business valuations there are some guidelines for using multipliers per market. The basic thought is that whenever there is more certainty about forecasting results based upon historical figures the higher the multiplier. An accounting firm with a steady base of long-time customers may expect that history will repeat itself over a longer period of time. But evidently there may be some discussion about choosing the right parameter and multiplier.

Advantages of a Rules of Thumb method:

1. Historical results are used in a market based setting.

2. Whenever a decision is made about parameter and multiplier the task of valuing is relatively easy.

3. Especially with ecommerce websites a rules of thumb method may be interesting as enough hard historical data is available to make the calculation. Combined with the more qualitative method based upon the 5 website value drivers it will give a good estimation of website worth.

4. Due to the use of multipliers this method is future orientated although it does not take into account the hidden factors of website strength or weakness.

Disadvantages of a Rules of Thumb method:
1. It may be difficult to choose the best possible parameter as the base of calculating value. The same goes for deciding upon the right multiplier.

2. There are many rules of thumbs to choose from and each will lead to a different estimated value.

3. However it uses a multiplier, it does not look at the driving forces of value of a website. It will only extrapolate historical results into the future without being aware of what really is going on with a particular website or ecommerce site.

So what to choose?
In my opinion there are 2 conditions you need to answer in choosing the most appropriate financial valuation method for your website.

1. **How much financial data is at hand?**
   Historical data and forecasted results are the main issue here. In general ecommerce websites may provide the needed historical data but in some cases results in the past could be very unstable due to the hectic of the online market place. This makes it harder to extrapolate historical data or make forecasts for the years to come.

2. **The financial impact of a possible deal**
   When you are buying or selling a relatively small website in matters of sales, leads, traffic or social impact than a rules of thumb approach may suffice to come to a value based upon a financial valuation. When a possible deal will have more financial weight it will be worthwhile to invest time and money in a thorough financial valuation.

In my opinion the best financial valuation method will be a Discounted Cash Flow method if you have access to all relevant financial data over a relatively long period of time (the last 5 to 6 years). Mind however that a small deviation of forecasted cash flow may result in a large positive or negative outcome. As we already discussed the challenge of attribution of results this implies that the DCF method is almost exclusively restricted for ecommerce website with a long track record.

An asset based valuation is in essence a good valuation method but it is not very useful in valuing the financial part of our website valuation process. In fact, the method I am introducing here in this book is a mix of an asset based and pure financial valuation. But here we will need the best possible financial valuation method for our website, the qualitative asset based approach will follow after this financial valuation phase.

I am not particularly fond of using a market based financial method in valuing a website or ecommerce website. The similarity this method needs just does not exist. Differences between websites, monetization, website value drivers and markets are just too large. But if you need a quick and very rough estimation of what a website could be worth it may trigger the conclusion of selling or buying a website. In that way reading about selling prices may be inspiring for the market (both sellers and buyers).

For smaller websites and ecommerce sites using a rule of thumb (or an average of 2 or 3 rules of thumbs) may be the right approach for this phase of the website valuation method I present here. What we need for now is a financial valuation based upon the financial results of our website. For many information based websites these results may be a bit greyish as attribution of leads to sales will be difficult. It does not make sense to apply a very thorough financial valuation method on a website where the basic data is flawed. Besides, in our next phase we will be looking under the hood to see how our website engine is humming. So we will adjust some shortcomings in our financial valuation method.

What if no financial data is available?

There are lots of websites out there that do not make any sales or profits, not even leads. Many of these sites provide information without any monetizing model active. They do not show ads nor generate leads for themselves or others so there are no tangible results to be attributed. Are these websites worthless? Of course not. Your house does not generate money, it only generates expenses, but it has a worth. The worth of a website that does not generate money is concentrated in the amount of organic traffic it generates. This traffic may not be tapped into yet, but that doesn't mean that it may not be overhauled into a money making machine.

For our general website valuation method this poses some problems however. We cannot start with phase 1, a financial valuation of these websites. So we have to skip this phase and go right to phase 2 where we will be looking at the internal powers that drive website value. It will make our work a little harder but at the end we will be able to make a valuation.

Further in this book I will explain how we can circumvent the absence of financial data in our website valuation process.

Now let's take a practical look at the complete process of website valuation.

Chapter 9: Website valuation in practice

Up to now we have talked about the process of website valuation in theory. We have discussed the importance of the 5 website value drivers, the step-by-step process of our website valuation method and the choice of financial valuation methods that represent phase 1 of the entire website valuation process. Now it is time to put theory into practice.

The best way of showing how the complete process works is by performing a website valuation based upon a fictitious website. You will see that the essence of valuing a website is a combination of calculation and judgement. This is no different from any other asset valuation process whether it be real estate, a business or a piece of art.

For our example we will take an ecommerce website with enough financial data to calculate a financial value. As I do not want to bother you with a thorough financial valuation based upon a DCF method we will use 2 rules of thumb methods. This financial valuation phase is not the essence of this book, there are many other sources around that can give you an in-depth insight in the practice of financial valuation methods. In fact I prefer to let this part of the valuation process be handled by a qualified accountant.

During the website valuation process described below I will inform you about all steps I take. So this is not a blueprint for a website valuation report, but it comes very close if you would skip the added information. When I perform a website valuation the comments are more thorough and there are more insights shared based upon real data and the website itself. The strengths and weaknesses described here sometimes fall out of the blue, that is intentional. I just want to show what kind of remarks you could be giving.

Our case

Website: www.241-shoes-and-sneakers-online-shop.com (fictitious website)

Year	Annual Sales (earnings)	Annual Net Profit
Year 1	$ 140.000,-	$ 20.000,-
Year 2	$ 300.000,-	$ 50.000,-
Year 3	$ 450.000,-	$ 80.000,-
Year 4	$ 550.000,-	$ 100.000,-
Year 5	$ 570.000,-	$ 85.000,-

Description website:

This ecommerce website is selling sporting shoes and sneakers to international markets. The main markets are the United States and the United Kingdom. All sales are coming from this website. The website has started 5 years ago and it has grown in sales and profits over the years.

Search Engine Optimization:

Active content marketing strategy. Each shoe is tested and reviewed.

Online advertising:

Active Google AdWords campaign aimed at the US and UK for specific brands and shoe types.

Costs of AdWords advertising:

Year	AdWords costs
Year 1	$ 20.000,-
Year 2	$ 40.000,-
Year 3	$ 70.000,-
Year 4	$ 100.000,-

Year 5	$ 120.000,-

Social media strategy:

Active on Facebook and Twitter, occasional on Snapchat.

We have access to Google Analytics, Google AdWords campaigns and all Social Media accounts.

Before we start

The information above is pretty basic of course. Normally we will need to know more about the business and website we are valuing. We do not have a visual of the website itself and we cannot go through all the statistics of Google Analytics. In the next steps I will add some fictitious data to show how we will walk through all the steps. Never mind this oversimplifying of the case at hand, the objective here is to show how a website valuation is executed. I do not want your focus to be deterred by adding too much specifics. So let's get started.

1] Financial valuation

In this case we use 2 rules of thumb, one focused on net profit, the other on earnings.

a} Earnings based rule of thumb:

Generally a multiplier of 0,75 to 1,5 is used based upon the average earnings figure of the last 4 to 5 years.

Average earnings:
(140.000 + 300.000 + 450.000 + 550.000 + 570.000) / 5 = $ 402.000,-

Choice of multiplier:
A tough question to begin with. It depends on the market, the

evolution of earnings and the risks involved what multiplier we will use. By multiplying past results we will take a shot at the future. But it is based upon historical financial data and we have not examined the underlying forces that drive website value. So here we will look at the evolution of earnings and mix it with common multipliers for specific markets. I must confess that this is a rather old-fashioned way of looking at market risk. In today's online world entry barriers for markets are much lower as we are operating in a truly global world where we will be constantly challenged by competitors that were not able to harm us in the days before the internet.

That being said, our market of sneakers is highly competitive and there are almost no entry barriers. Looking at the earnings evolution we will see a nice uptick although growth is not as exuberant as in the first years.

All things considered we will use a multiplier of 0,8.

Applying this multiplier to our earnings average will lead to the following financial value:

$ 402.000,- x 0,8 = $ 321.600,-

b} Net Profit based rule of thumb

In general a multiplier between 4 to 6 is being used on the average net profit obtained in the preceding years.

Average net profit:
(20.000 + 50.000 + 80.000 + 100.000 + 85.000) / 5 = $ 67.000,-

Choice of multiplier:

Again a challenge. Picking the right multiplier for this net profit rule of thumb is generally based upon the evolution of net profit and the market this website is operating in. It remains a matter of good judgement which multiplier to choose.

Looking at the evolution of net profit here and the highly competitive market we will go for a rather conservative multiplier of 4.

When we apply this multiple to our average net profit we will get the following financial value based upon this Net Profit rule of thumb:

$ 67.000,- x 4 = $ 268.000,-

So we now have 2 different values based upon 2 different rules of thumb. I can assure you that this is always the case. In many cases financial valuations based upon earnings rules of thumbs are higher than those based upon net profit. Then again, net profit is a more complex result than earnings. Net profit may be manipulated in either way (too positive or too negative). Earnings are a bit more straightforward.

Mixing the two results

If I ever use a rules of thumbs method I always try to use 2 or 3 several rules and average the results. If we would apply that here we will get the following value:

($ 321.600,- + $ 268.000,-) / 2 = $ 294.800,-

By using 2 rules of thumb methods we could value our website at more or less $ 294.800,-.

Before we move on we will let this sink in. What did we do? We used historic financial results as our base of calculation and we've extrapolated these results into the future. Does this make sense? Yes, it does from a financial point of view. It is like buying a used car and looking at its mileage and regular service checks. If the mileage is relatively low and service checks have been executed we should be buying a great car. For most cars this seems good enough. If you buy a well-known brand of car with a good reputation, mileage and servicing are the variables. But with a website it is a bit different. There is not one single website that is completely similar to the other. The results may be the same but the origin of these results has been left out of the picture, yet. Suppose all cars are hand-built by different constructors, brands do not exist. Would you be contented with mileage and service checks as your reference points? Or would you prefer someone to look under the hood and check its engine? That is what we will do in the second phase of our website valuation process. Let's put on our overalls, we will encounter some grease and oil and maybe some rusty parts.

2] Qualitative valuation

In phase 2 of our website valuation process we will gauge the 5 website value drivers of this website. Before we will plunge into the engine of our website I have to make a very important remark.

What we are looking for are the **extra** strengths or weaknesses within our website that add or subtract value from the value derived from our financial valuation. Let us not forget that within the financial valuation process we have extrapolated historic **financial** results to future value. What we have seen in researching these 5 website value drivers is that they forecast future value in a way that they have not yet have been materialized in historic results. If we would only extrapolate historic financial results we would be losing out on the values (positive or negative) these 5 factors will add.

So let us now continue with the qualitative valuation of the website at hand.

Our starting point for this qualitative phase is the outcome of the previous part of this process, the financial value. In our case that is a mixed average between 2 rules of thumb but of course this may also be a value based upon a DCF or CoE method.

Our starting value here is: $ 294.800,-

Before we start

We are about to take a look at each single website value driver. But first we must take a broader view. As we have access to Analytics and data about advertising, social media, conversions and financial data we need to take time to suck it all in. I personally begin with going through all important pages of the website, then I will go through Analytics and financial data and finally I will go through data of advertising and social media platforms.

By doing that I will get a good and thorough understanding of the website and why it performs like it does. It is like planning a trip to a city like Paris. You inform yourself of sights you want to see, their historical background, means of transportation to get there and so forth.

By taking this broader view and occasionally dig in a bit deeper you will learn what makes this website tick. It is important to know this before our first task: assigning weighting factors to our website value drivers.

Assigning weighting factors to the 5 website value drivers

As we have discussed in chapter 6 we would normally assign these weighting factors to our website value drivers:

Website Value Driver:	Weighting factor
Organic strength	30%
Online authority strength	25%
Advertising & social media strength	20%
Conversion strength	15%
Technical strength	10%

Our first question is whether these multiples make sense to this particular website and market. As this website is operating in a highly competitive international market and AdWords is a very important part of our marketing effort I would raise the weighting of Advertising & Social Strength with 5%. For the same reasons I would lower the Online Authority Strength weighting with 5% as this market is so fragmented and the brands offered are more important than the website brand.

With that in mind I would use the following weighting factors for this website:

Website Value Driver:	Weighting factor
Organic strength	30%
Online authority strength	20%
Advertising & social media strength	25%
Conversion strength	15%
Technical strength	10%

Our objective: determining the right multiplier for each website value driver

Now we will go through each and every website value driver trying to establish its relative strength or weakness. Our objective is to translate this relative strength or weakness into a single multiplier for that website value driver. We will look for extra added or subtracted value that has not yet fully materialized into the results that shaped the value of our financial estimation.

As we are dealing with an online shop where financial data about revenue, profits and costs are available and transparent we have to put more emphasis on the value of our financial valuation. That is why I always put a limit on the impact of the qualitative valuation in these situations. For me this limit lies within the bandwidth of a multiplier of minimum 0,5 and maximum 1,5 for ecommerce sites.

If we did not have enough financial data or arbitrary data or even non-existent data we can go beyond these limits or even work with absolute money amounts.

In cases where the financial valuation phase is carried out with more emphasis on future results we may want to diminish the impact of our qualitative valuation even further. This could be the case when you are dealing with an ecommerce website with steady financial data and a financial valuation method that is both reliable and very future-based like a Discounted Cash Flow method. But, and this is an important but, if the DCF method is based upon a forecasted cash flow report that is not thorough enough or future cash flows are solely based upon extrapolations of historic cash flows we cannot narrow the bandwidth of our multipliers. My advice: always try to find out how the financial valuation has been carried out.

For this ecommerce site we will stick to the multiplier bandwidth of 0,5 to 1,5. Now let's get started with our qualitative valuation process!

Website Value Driver 1:
Organic strength
The basis for this analysis is your statistical web package, in this case we will use the insights of Google Analytics. What do we need to gauge the organic strength of a website? We need to:

1. Understand the business the website is operating in
2. Have an overall view on the evolution of organic traffic
3. Apply the right analytical approach in measuring organic strength
4. Make an all-encompassing judgement

Let us walk through these 4 steps to determine organic strength.

1] The market for sneakers and sporting shoes

We do not need to know all the ins and outs of a particular market. What we need to know is whether a market is relatively closed or open for competition. This depends on the market situation. Some markets are dominated by only a handful of players due to large entry barriers, some are open to everyone with a website. It also depends on whether you own or have exclusive rights for a well-established brand.

As we said before, competition in the sneakers markets is huge. There is a large supply of online shops offering more or less the same brands of sneakers at more or less the same prices. There is not much room for lowering retail prices to let the low price drives sales. The same goes for putting large amounts of money in establishing a preferred shopping brand by advertising massively (and remain a healthy margin). In other words there is little room for heavy shop-brand promotion while at the same time run a profitable business.

Getting the right traffic into your shop (the traffic that is seeking the shoes you sell) at the lowest possible cost is crucial in this market. It goes without saying that triggering free organic traffic is very important in making sales and nice profit margins. That is why we have awarded this website value driver with a high 30% weighting factor.

2] The evolution of organic traffic

This is an important part of our organic strength measurement. How is organic traffic evolving through time? A very healthy evolution would be to see continuing growth in the amount of organic traffic our website attracts. Of course when organic traffic is declining our verdict would be negative.

How do I judge the organic evolution of a website?

Generally I will go back for 5 years if possible and divide these years in periods of 6 months. I start with the most recent whole month that traffic is recorded and I will go back in steps of 6 months. Why 6 months? Because this period is small enough to grasp the evolution and large enough to filter out holiday seasons and other disturbing effects such as a temporary seasonal slowdown in search volumes. Of course with highly seasonal markets you always will notice the impact on organic traffic, that is no problem as it should occur within the same 6 months each year and you still will be able to deduct the overall evolution.

With our sneakers website we come up with the following organic traffic breakdown:

6 month period	Organic traffic	Relative change compared to previous period
01/05/year 1 – 31/10/year 1	22.500	
01/11/year 1 – 30/04/year 2	24.900	+ 11%
01/05/year 2 – 31/10/year 2	45.600	+ 83%
01/11/year 2 – 30/04/year 3	56.800	+ 25%
01/05/year 3 – 31/10/year 3	65.200	+ 15%
01/11/year 3 – 30/04/year 4	88.500	+ 36%
01/05/year 4 – 31/10/year 4	125.300	+ 42%
01/11/year 4 – 30/04/year 5	166.900	+ 33%

What we are seeing here is a slow but steady growth of organic traffic in the first year, a strong growth of organic traffic during 2015 and the early part of 2016 and an exuberant growth in the last year. The relative growth is slowing down in the last 6 months but we must keep in mind that in absolute terms growth is still very significant.

Looking at these figures the evolution of organic growth is very healthy indeed. But before we make decisions about organic strength we have to dig a little deeper into our website and the drivers of organic growth itself.

3] Analyzing organic traffic data

Growth in organic traffic sounds great but what are the reasons for this growth and what about the results this traffic generates? Here we will look at the heart of the matter of organic traffic.

The first thing I'll do is analyzing the pages that trigger organic traffic. I will look at the total number of pages and the kind of pages that are responsible for organic traffic and organic growth. The larger the number of pages that trigger organic traffic the healthier the website. Suppose you have a website with 500 pages and 400 of them attract organic traffic what does this tell you? In general you could say that this means that most of your webpages are well-indexed and offer the right content for a wide variety of search queries. It is a very strong signal that not only your website is performing well on organic up to now, it also hints very strongly to the future. A website with many of its pages performing well on organic traffic will not be pushed away quickly from search engines' results pages.

Then we will have to look at these pages that outperform other pages in triggering organic traffic. What are these pages? Are they content-based pages, ecommerce pages or do they cater to specific search queries. It is also important to look at the numbers. If only a handful of pages trigger the bulk of organic traffic it is important to know what these pages are and you may want to judge their vulnerability. I have come across poorly made SEO pages that were attracting organic traffic for only a month or two and then vanished from the organic leaderboard.

I also want to know whether Search Engine Optimization is carried out and to what extent. Have SEO activities centered around content or technical optimizations or where black hat SEO techniques used. Unsurprisingly I favor content-based optimizations over manipulating techniques.

4] Making your final judgement on organic strength

In order to put an absolute multiple on organic strength I make a score card of strengths and weaknesses. By doing that you will be able to make a better judgement. Let's do it for this fictitious sneakers-website. The remarks below are, of course, also fictitious.

Strengths:

1. Evolution of organic growth looks very healthy. The engine of organic growth is fully on steam.

2. Almost 75% of all pages attract organic traffic. This means that most of the pages contribute to organic traffic.

3. 15 of the Top 25 pages that attract the most organic traffic are content pages. This website has begun building content pages in 2016 and this strategy is working out fine. There are still numerous chances in writing and adding more content pages so the future looks bright.

4. Search Engine Optimization is concerned around adding high quality content. A freelance SEO specialist is helping to generate content and using the right white-

hat SEO techniques.

5. URL structures are optimized within the content pages.

6. The web domain is old enough to be out of the danger zone of search engines. This means that traffic results become more predictable than is the case with relatively new web domains.

Weaknesses:

1. Although organic growth is healthy, relative growth is stagnating. Of course we must take into account that in absolute terms growth is still taking up and it is always more difficult to grow a larger base than a smaller one. But still, it seems like we are hitting a wall of growth in the near future.

2. Ecommerce pages underperform in organic growth. The growth of last 2 years can be attributed for a great part to the adding of new content pages. This indicates that we must keep on adding content pages that are more laborious than adding new ecommerce pages with new products. There still are different options in adding new content pages such as pages that compare 2 different types of sneakers and brand pages that give in-depth background of brands sold. Still we do not know whether these new approaches will add the traffic we were used to.

Final judgement on organic strength

Based upon the above conclusions I attribute a multiplier of 1,4 to organic strength. The strengths of organic traffic absolutely weigh out the organic weaknesses and it is to be expected that organic traffic will still rise significantly in the years to come.

Final result:

Multiplier: 1,4

Weighting factor: 30%

Website Value Driver 2:
Online authority strength

Online authority plays a major role in garnering future website value. It is in itself an engine for website traffic, mainly organic, direct and referral traffic. The essence of online authority is that it raises the bar for competitors to take away business from your online activities. The more online authority a website has the easier it is to translate your strategies into results. Online authority is like an underlying current that feeds your website. There is one problem, it is hard to measure.

Of all the 5 website value drivers online authority is the less tangible. There is no single online authority statistic, but that is also one of its powers. It drives traffic and results from all sorts of sources and in all sorts of ways. I have come across many websites from market leaders. Looking at the data of their websites I saw the following:

- High conversion rates from new visitors
- Relatively large volumes emanating from organic traffic within its niche
- Lots of referral traffic from important sources
- Lots of branded traffic (keywords with the name of the website or company included)
- Lots of traffic coming from email or newsletters

So in order to gauge the online authority strength I will turn my attention again at data from Analytics. I will also use a keyword tool.

Turning back at our fictitious website www.241-shoes-and-sneakers-online-shop.com we came up with the following (fictitious) conclusions:

Strengths:

1. Using our keyword tool we notice that keyword combinations with "241 shoes" and "241 sneakers" are typed in more and more during the last year. The absolute volume of these branded keywords is however still small. It seems like our brand is on the rise.

2. The number of newsletter subscribers is rising steadily. Within the last year we saw the increase stepping up. The growth of new subscribers is 55% against the previous year, a sharp incline compared to 35% the previous year. We also notice that unsubscriptions fell with 40%. A healthy sign for a brand on the move.

3. Organic traffic and organic growth is very substantial as we have seen in the previous website value driver. Although by far the most of organic traffic is emanating from webpages that are catered to specific search queries around our niche (and not from branded search queries), it shows that search engines are treating our website content as authoritative. An important sign for online authority.

Weaknesses:

1. Referral traffic is not substantial. The volume of referral traffic lags other sources as Organic, Direct and Social Media. Taking a deeper look at the backgrounds of referral traffic we see 5 major traffic generators mainly coming from banners we placed on shoe-blogs. There

are not much referrals coming from other websites within our niche. This is a bit troublesome as our website has to offer lots of high quality content. Search engines acknowledge our content, other niche players do not for the moment. I must add that getting backlinks from websites within a very competitive market is not that easy as it used to be in the early years of the internet. They do not want to lose traffic to other parties. Even more importantly, most of the websites that are active in our niche have their own monetizing program which hampers outgoing links.

2. Conversion rates for new visitors is still 30% lower than from returning visitors (not customers, but visitors). This percentage is steady during the last 3 years. Somehow people need more time to get acquainted with our brand. This is a sign that our brand of 241 shoes is still not removing buying thresholds.

Final judgement on authority strength

Based upon the above conclusions I attribute a multiplier of 1,1 to authority strength. It is clear that this website still has much ground to cover before being a real top-of-mind website and brand. The positive part is the way search engines are looking at our website. In many cases they are ahead of the market. This website is definitely moving in the right direction in building online authority, but we aren't there yet.

Final result:

Multiplier: 1,1

Weighting factor: 20%

Website Value Driver 3:
Advertising & social media strength

Here we will focus on the advertising and social media strategy behind our website. For me exploiting a social media strategy is the same as advertising, even when you are not paying for social media traffic directly you will pay for it by investing time and energy. Of course you could say the same about active SEO but there are some important differences I cannot explain here without boring you to death. Well, all right, I give you two differences: one is that a social media strategy is aimed at driving traffic from a third party website where you are not in control as you are on your own website. The other is that SEO is an investment into your website with long term returns whereas social media traffic is often more short-termed focused with direct results. But as I said before we can discuss these differences more thoroughly but that would be a bit besides the central theme of this book.

If you ever have been involved in advertising a website you will know how difficult it is to run an effective campaign that is structurally running a positive return on investment. In the good old days before the internet measuring the results of your advertising efforts was extremely difficult. There were agencies who could tell you that everything was going fine, but to be honest, most of them were as clueless about results as the advertiser.

Today we can measure the results of our online campaigns much better, not perfect as some people like to tell you. Attributions of engagements to orders or leads is still not 100% proof and it probably will never reach that point but we are able to tell whether our efforts are worth the cost or not.

Why is it so important to have an effective online advertising campaign running for your website? Wouldn't it be better to just do without advertising and solely rely on organic traffic? Well, it is not, you would abstain yourself of a profitable traffic channel, if managed properly of course. Putting it in other words, an effective advertising campaign is like a money machine. You will put $ 1,- in this machine and it will give you $1,20 or $ 1,50 back. Great isn't it? Yes, but there are numerous campaigns out there that are more like an inverted money machine, you'll put $ 1,- in it and you will get back 50 cents. Going to the casino would be a better option (and much more fun with drinks on the house).

But suppose your website would be running a structural profitable online advertising campaign, wouldn't that be a great asset? My findings are even stronger, if a website is operating a campaign with a positive return on investment it not only has a very large chance of staying profitable for years to come, in many cases it would even become more profitable. How could this be true? We have to look for the reason why a campaign is running so effectively. I found the following reasons:

1. **Not much competition within the niche**
   In some markets there is not that much competition. Comes as a surprise maybe but I personally have come across several markets where the pie is sliced between a handful of competitors and some didn't even bother to operate a solid online strategy. In some cases you will find these markets in very small niches or markets that allow specific technical skills but I must confess that my own experiences were in very large global markets with huge turnovers and even bigger profits. There are many global markets out there that are dominated by a couple of competitors who have established so much power in their markets that they even do not need to advertise, or so they think, because I always proved them wrong...

   When one of such companies is trying out online advertising it almost immediately turns profitable. You

can steal away market share from competitors even by advertising on competitors brands and products. And of course click prices are generally low as competition is sleeping.
But to be honest, the bulk of my customers are active in moderate or highly competitive markets. They have to pull different strings to obtain a profitable advertising campaign.

2. **Optimization techniques that eventually lead to an effective campaign**
In all other than the above mentioned situation this is really the only reason why an online advertising or social media campaign turns in the results you are after. Okay, I have come across advertising campaigns that were profitable from day 1 without bothering about optimizations but it never lasted. In most cases campaigns turn positive after continuous improvements and optimizations. During that process a win-win is occurring: you will not only see results spike up but you will learn why it does.

That knowledge will be the basis of your future growth in managing your online advertising or social media campaigns. That doesn't mean that it will be a straight line up to the moon. It even doesn't mean that your results will always be positive. Online advertising and social media platforms are constantly changing as well as competition within your market and do not forget the bottom line of these platforms you are working with. They too will optimize your advertising efforts, to their advantage. But all in all, when you have an online advertising campaign that is running structurally profitable you have the best papers inn hand to keep on running this campaign profitable.

Does it make a difference who is running your campaign, an outside agency or an internal department? That depends on what is being sold, the website or the company. Sometimes it is better to have an external agency that may be transferred to the new owners, in other situations the internal know-how may be kept in place. But in general it does not matter much, as you will be transferring a structural positive campaign it is much easier to maintain than a structural negative campaign that loses money. Remember, we are valuing the website as of now with a look at the future. Our valuation is not based upon what the new owner will do with it.

Now we leave these side comments for what they are and we will focus our attention again to our sneakers website.

Social media results:

Here we will be looking at traffic and conversions generated from social media. We saw the following results:

Social Media	Traffic Social Media last 6 months	Rise or fall compared to previous 6 months	Conversion % last 6 months
Facebook	12.500	+ 20%	0,4%
Snapchat	11.800	+ 40%	0,3%
Instagram	10.700	+ 30%	0,4%
Pinterest	7.600	+ 30%	2,1%
YouTube	2.800	+ 5%	0,7%
Twitter	600	- 30%	0,3%
Google+	800	- 40%	0,5%

Total	46.800		

Of course you can go back further in time to see how traffic and conversions have evolved over time. In the ever-changing world of social media I would not go back further than 2 to 3 years. These platforms are not that stable in driving traffic and conversions. The same goes for extrapolating past results. I am always more conservative with social media results than with Google AdWords traffic as you are more in control with the latter.

Our other advertising tool consists of a Google AdWords Search + Shopping campaign.

Google Ads results:

Here we will take into account a wider spread of results. In most cases I consider the results of the last 3 years, divided in periods of 6 months.

6 month period	Google Ads Search Traffic	Google Ads Search conversion %	Google Ads Shopping Traffic	Google Ads Shopping conversion %
01/05/year 1 – 31/10/year 1	22.500	0,8%		
01/11/year 1 – 30/04/year 2	24.900	1,1%		
01/05/year 2 – 31/10/year 2	45.600	1,2%		
01/11/year 2 – 30/04/year 3	56.800	1,0%	35.000	1,5%
01/05/year 3 – 31/10/year	65.200	1,5%	54.400	1,7%

3				
01/11/year 3 – 30/04/year 4	88.500	1,8%	85.800	2,3%
01/05/year 4 – 31/10/year 4	125.300	2,1%	87.000	2,1%
01/11/year 4 – 30/04/year 5	166.900	2,4%	92.000	2,2%

Google Shopping campaigns are more automated than Search campaigns are with a result that less optimizations are needed. That does not imply that Shopping campaigns cannot be optimized, on the contrary, there are major gains to achieve in obstructing certain keywords and optimizing the products within your feed (skipping product feeds that do not convert). But in general in Google Ads Search there are many more optimizations you can utilize.

Now let us go through the pros and cons of our advertising and social media efforts.

Strengths:

1. An active social media strategy is being implemented. Every day there is interaction on most social media platforms. New shoes are being promoted and links to the relevant web pages are shared.

2. Social media traffic is still growing although conversion rates are still on the low side with the exception of Pinterest and YouTube.

3. Up to now all social media traffic is "free", which means that no paid social media campaigns are being

operated.

4. Google Ads has been set up for most product categories and results are reported on a monthly basis. Optimizations are made within the company supported by a professional Google Ads specialist. Each month this specialist will discuss the optimizations carried out by a dedicated marketeer within the company. This is a perfect way to build up Google Ads know-how in house and making sure that there is always a professional back-up when it is needed (in case the in house professional gets sick or will quit the job).

5. Conversions of Google Ads are going up on a structural basis. With a current conversion rate of more than 2% it is performing well and there is still room for an uptick in the future.

6. Since 2 years ROI of Google Ads is positive. Even more important, by increasing the daily budget in recent years ROI remained positive and even went up. A very healthy sign of a well-run campaign.

7. Google Ads Search and Shopping campaigns only have been running within the United States. There is lots of room to expand the campaign to other countries although this will probably have a negative impact on short term ROI.

Weaknesses:

1. Conversions rates of social media are relatively low. You could say that this is no problem as every conversion counts but in this case it keeps 1 person very busy managing these accounts on a daily basis.

This is an in house job but it takes 3 to 4 hours a day.

2. The results of the Google Ads campaigns, although very positive, have been for 100% attributable to 1 region, the USA. Not all things learnt may be carried over to other geographical locations if one would consider to expand the AdWords efforts.

3. Up to now the decision has been made not to run paid advertising campaigns on social media. Maybe that has been a good decision but we cannot say that for sure. However, we did not gain any insights either.

Final judgement on advertising and social media strength

Based upon the above conclusions I attribute a multiplier of 1,3 to this website value driver. It is most certainly a big plus that the Google Ads campaigns are running a positive ROI. Moreover it is clear that optimizations have been fruitful and beyond any doubt it has been an instructive ride with gains made on the knowledge level. Social media efforts are not that positive still.

The time and energy spent on sharing valuable information is relatively considerable compared to the results. There is still lots of room in expanding Google Ads efforts within the US and outside. The insights gained will come in very handy.

Final result:

Multiplier: 1,3

Weighting factor: 25%

Website Value Driver 4:
Conversion strength

Conversion is all about turning traffic into results. These results may vary among different websites, here our main focus is driving sales. In some cases you can distinguish major and minor conversions. A major conversion would be a direct sale, a minor one could be anything like a newsletter subscription, an abandoned shopping cart or a product sheet download. In valuing a website I generally will focus on 1 single major conversion. Here it will be the direct sale of sneakers.

What we are looking for is how well our website is able to convert traffic into sales. Of course this is somewhat arbitrary. It depends on the type of conversion and the market you are in what may be labelled a good or bad conversion rate. On the other hand there are some benchmarks to use.

There is intensive discussion about what comprises a good, average or below average conversion rate. Some say a conversion rate of 3% or higher is good and around 2% is average. Again, it all depends on the market and of course the type of conversion you are rating. In general I use a 2% to 2,5% rate as a general benchmark, but I will always make a remark about it. In some cases a conversion rate below 1,5% is still good. It also depends on the type of traffic you are attracting. Say you operate a very popular blog about investing on the stock markets and the only conversion you offer is a book you wrote about investments, the conversion rate will be much lower than an online shop that offers a broad range of sneakers like this ecommerce site we are dealing with.

So how will I go about gauging conversion strength?

I will be looking at the following metrics:

1. **The type of conversion measured**
   It makes a big difference what kind of conversion you measure. With ecommerce websites it is pretty common to measure website sales but in some cases website owners prefer to measure shopping cart additions. This may make sense when paid conversions will get lost in Analytics due to a bad alignment of conversions by payment providers.

   But of course, a paid conversion is of a higher order than a shopping cart addition. The same goes for measuring sales in Dollars or Euro's compared to measuring items sold (where each ordered item will account for 1 conversion however small or big the order in a Dollar or Euro amount will be).

   With lead generating websites the challenge may be even bigger. Do we count all soft leads or do we have a system in place that makes a distinction between soft leads and hard ones? So in appraising the relative conversion strength we must take into account the type of conversion whether it be a hard or softer conversion.

2. **The different conversion rates divided among traffic sources**
   I will look at the total conversion rate for each different traffic source or channel and I will compare the results. Conversion rates of organic origin for instance are often higher than for referral traffic. Within organic traffic you will often find a bunch of branded keywords (comprising of your own brand, company name or website). This is especially true for well-known ecommerce sites (and

not so with blogs).

3. **The evolution of conversions**
   Are conversion rates going up or down in time? An important way of looking at the relative health of conversions. It may show the efforts in conversion optimization or the building of our online brand (people tend to buy more easily with established websites or brands).

In gauging the relative strength of our website in converting traffic to leads, orders or sales we must start with the type of conversion measured and then go through conversion rates divided among traffic channels and evolution in time. Let's give an example based upon our sneakers website.

With our sneakers website conversions are measured as sales in Dollar amounts (ecommerce transactions in Analytics). This makes perfect sense as our margins do not differ much among different shoes. For our analysis I prefer to look at conversion ratios instead of conversions in absolute terms (or Dollar terms).

We can break down the following conversion rates among channels:

6 month period	Conversion rates per traffic channel				
	Organic	AdWords	Direct traffic	Referrals	Social Media
01/05/year 1	1,5%	0,8%	1,3%	0,2%	0,1%

Period					
– 31/10/year 1					
01/11/year 1 – 30/04/year 2	1,4%	1,1%	1,6%	0,4%	0,1%
01/05/year 2 – 31/10/year 2	1,7%	1,2%	2,0%	0,8%	0,3%
01/11/year 2 – 30/04/year 3	1,7%	1,2%	2,0%	1,0%	0,2%
01/05/year 3 – 31/10/year 3	1,8%	1,6%	2,4%	0,9%	0,2%
01/11/year 3 – 30/04/year 4	2,1%	2,0%	2,6%	1,0%	0,3%
01/05/year 4 – 31/10/year 4	2,0%	2,1%	2,5%	1,1%	0,2%
01/11/year 4 – 30/04/year 5	2,2%	2,3%	2,7%	1,2%	0,3%

Here we have only supplied a table of conversion rates as we already saw a steady uptick of absolute traffic among different channels. In most cases I would also mention the absolute number of conversions as the conversion ratio may be higher while the total number of conversions could be lower. Here that is not the case as we saw traffic move up among all channels.

Again, you could dig a bit deeper into the evolution of conversions but that is not the point of this book. I cannot supply a complete Analytics report here without boring you to the hilt.

Strengths:

1. Conversion rates show a structural upward move. This is most certainly a very healthy sign for future conversion expectations.

2. The high traffic channels such as organic and paid traffic report the highest conversions.

3. Conversions of paid traffic also show a steady improvement. Even more importantly AdWords traffic is converting in accordance with organic traffic. As AdWords traffic can be stepped up easily (also in new international markets) this gives rise to a possible powerful boost of sales if applied wisely.

Weaknesses:

1. Although conversion rates show a steady move upward they still are a bit feeble for an ecommerce website in sneakers. You would expect rates around 2,5% to maybe 3% for some channels. Of course this is a high competition market where people tend to compare prices of shoes among different contenders but as prices from our website are not higher than average, conversions could be higher.

2. Direct traffic has the highest conversion rates which is a normal thing (not always as branded search finds its way also to the organic channel). Again you would expect a higher conversion ratio here. That being said it seems to pick up momentum.

Final judgement on conversion strength

Conversion rates are going up. To understand the underlying reasons why this ratio is moving in an upward direction cannot be concluded right away. To tackle this we should ask questions about strategies. If prices have been cut conversions could go up. So we need to dig into this. If we can eliminate price cuts or selling below a healthy margin we can look to conversion optimization strategies carried out or at a more simpler but even more positive effect that materializes when a brand is gaining more trustworthiness or comes into popular demand. Here margins have remained steady during the last years so our conversion plus comes from more structural and healthy sources. It goes too far to make a fictitious remark about the real reason of this uptick but in real life one should address this issue with the website owner or management.

Although conversion rates show a healthy movement we still underperform a bit on the average conversion rate. But we may expect that rates will go up even further as our store brand will become more popular in the future.

I would attribute a multiplier of 1,2 for conversion strength as the positive (conversion rate growth) outperforms the negative (a relatively average total conversion rate).

Final result:

Multiplier:	1,2
Weighting factor:	15%

Website Value Driver 5:
Technical strength

In the early years of the internet we were all limited in access through the lack of band width and speed. Websites in those days had to be simple to be loaded rapidly. The use of images was always a challenge as many users were not able to see them, let alone videos. Today speed and band width have accelerated immensely. Images, video's, live streaming, it is no problem at al for most part of the world (not all mind you). That does not imply that we can do whatever we like with our websites. Page loading is still an issue and the same goes for making sure that your website will be easily accessed and viewed by mobile devices. More importantly is a well-managed and secure website making sure that your website is not easily hacked.

Another big issue is the design and functionality of your website. Although some may say that web design is a subjective esthetical issue I have to disagree on that. Yes, people may disagree about the look & feel of a website but there are websites that use an outdated design that may have worked in the past but is not up to date anymore. It is a bit like car design, the older models will stand out like "old" and the new models like "new" whether you like them or not.

In judging the technical strength of a website I take in the following issues:

- a) Loading time of website/webpages
- b) Mobile friendliness
- c) Functionality, easy access to al major pages, user friendliness
- d) Website design, look & feel
- e) Order process with ecommerce websites

Why do we bother to look at the technical strength of a website? Because it may have an impact on future results. In most cases we can prevent a negative impact by keeping our website up-to-date on all major issues but it comes at a cost. Sometimes we need to alter the design or put a new website in place. Besides paying for a new website it also may impact future results as we may lose substantial volumes of traffic if this process is not being carried out with care (and even then you may lose organic traffic, even with all redirects in place).

If we only take a look at the results up to now without acknowledging risk and costs for new web designs, maintenance, updates and potential traffic losses we would delude ourselves.

With our fictitious website we could come up with the following strengths and weaknesses:

Strengths:

1. Although not opted for a specific mobile site the website is mobile friendly for all pages. The mobile ordering process is easy and user friendly.

2. The website platform used is a Magento platform. This open source platform may be maintained and updated by numerous web designers so there is no dependency upon a single web design bureau.

3. In the past years there were no significant security issues nor hosting issues. HTTPS is installed and no major issues occurred although conversions were not being measured for 2 months. Now this is fixed.

Weaknesses:

1. Loading time for the mobile version is under average. For the desktop version it is just above average. There is a need to fix this in the coming months.

2. A new update to the latest Magento version is planned for this year. This may have an impact on traffic as some URL's may alter (although this should not be necessary if closely watched).

Final judgement on technical strength:

Here we have only mentioned some issues. Of course there could be numerous smaller issues that could be taken into account. Whenever I am valuing a major website I will call in advice from a technical web designer. He or she is better suited to really dig into the serious matters and add some useful insights.

For this website I would give positive marks but of course it is just an example.

Final result:

Multiplier: 1,2

Weighting factor: 10%

3] Calculating the total weighted multiplier

After weighing and attributing each website value driver we can calculate a total multiplier based upon our qualitative analysis.

Website Value Driver:	Weighting factor	Multiplier	Weighted Multiplier
Organic strength	30%	1,4	0,42
Online authority strength	20%	1,1	0,22
Advertising & social media strength	25%	1,3	0,325
Conversion strength	15%	1,2	0,18
Technical strength	10%	1,2	0,12
Total Weighted Multiplier:			**1,265**

Our total weighted multiplier is 1,265. That will be the calculated multiplier to use on the value that resulted from our financial valuation.

4] Final website valuation

Up to now we have a value obtained from our financial valuation and we have attributed weightings and multipliers in our qualitative valuation. Now we can put the 2 together and come up with a final Dollar amount that will give us the estimated worth of this website.

Here is what it adds up to:

Financial Valuation: $ 294.800,-

Qualitative Valuation Multiplier: 1,265

Total estimated value: $ 294.800,- x 1,265 = $ 372.922,-

The value of this website has an estimated worth of $ 372.922,-

So now we have completed a website valuation for our fictitious website. Of course in reality you can come up with much more detail and backgrounds. I refrained from doing that here. Otherwise we would go way to far on our fictitious path. What I wanted to show you are the broad outlines of a website valuation process. Again, valuing a website is not a computerized system where you can put in a couple of data and expect to come up with a final Dollar or Euro amount. You must judge a website on its merits, the method described above will guide you through this process, but you still have to use your own brain power.

Chapter 10: Valuing a website without ecommerce activities

What if there are no ecommerce activities? If your website does not sell products or services online does such a website have a worth to be calculated? The answer is yes of course. In essence every website has a worth although there are numerous websites that are worth practically nothing. There are also many websites that do not sell anything online but are worth significant sums of money. That leads us to the tricky part of the question, how to estimate the worth of such websites when you cannot calculate with hard numbers like sales or profits?

Let us first distinguish a number of websites that are non-ecommerce websites. Here are some examples:

1. **Information based websites that sell advertising space**
   Think of blogs and online newspapers or publishers. A large part of the internet is occupied by these types of websites and they attract the bulk of online traffic. Just think of how many times a day you browse to one or more of your favorite news sites.

2. **Lead generating company websites**
   In both B2C and B2B markets you will come across a large variety of information based websites that focus on communicating their products and services in order to attract their target audience. Their main goal is to convert website traffic into sales and marketing leads or visits to their off line shops. Various lead generation options are available: online contact forms, white paper downloads, online chats and of course the old-

fashioned but ever effective telephone call.

3. **Online community websites**
   There are millions of online communities and online fora that attract visitors in droves. Of course we all know the usual suspects of social media and they either sell advertisements or paid extra features but there are many other smaller social media that do not have a sophisticated monetizing system in place. The same goes for many online fora that keep discussions going on about products, services or persons without really selling you something directly online.

4. **Platforms**
   Lots of websites are platforms or market places that offer free or paid advertising space to consumers or businesses. In essence nothing is being sold directly, otherwise it would be an ecommerce website. In many cases advertisers have to pay the platform but in some cases it is all for free. Of course job boards also fall into this category.

5. **Search engines and directories**
   Google isn't the only search engine around. There are numerous websites that offer a search or directory function. Some offer a free service, some have a monetized system working either in paid listings or advertisements.

I am sure you could come up with even different website types that do not run a direct online shop. The internet is teeming with websites that offer information or a specific answer to a need without offering a direct paid product or service. How can we make a solid valuation of these types of websites? In order to do that we need a different approach. Instead of solely looking at the website itself I prefer to take into account the intentions of the buying party or, when there isn't a party available, I will try to look through the eyes of a possible buying candidate. But our 5 website value drivers remain important.

Let us look at how we can tackle this challenge. I will introduce 2 ways of valuing non-ecommerce websites:

A] The attribution method

Phase 1: Valuing and attributing the current money stream

Phase 2: Financial valuation

Phase 3: Assessing the strength of our 5 website value drivers

B] The possible buyer method

A] The attribution method

Phase 1: Valuing and attributing the current money stream

The first question we have to ask ourselves is this: What is the purpose of our website in relation with the financial goals of our organization? It is important to focus our attention to the money objectives of our website or company. The second question will be this: what will be the contribution of our website with regard to these financial goals? We have to establish an attribution method that tells us what percentage of our total sales or profits may be attributed to our online impact.

If we own a B2B company that is selling industrial products to a specific target group of let's say oil drilling platforms our website would provide information about our products and services and the money objective will be the sale of these products and services. That is the money objective of the company and website, all is aimed at selling our products and services. But what part of our sales originates of our website and online strategy? We can use lead generation systems within our CRM tools that may provide an answer to this question. We can use Analytics or other statistical packages that supply information about lead generation forms completed and we can use off line administration tools.

The better we administer the touch points that will lead up to our final conversions (selling our industrial products and services) the more accurate the attribution method will be. In the end we want to come up with an attribution method that shows us the percentage of the turnover that leads back to our website or online strategy. In some cases a multi-layered attribution model would be our best pick. It is perfectly possible that the first contact or touch point would be made through the website (due to content marketing efforts) and that finally our sales team will close the deal. We have to take into account these different touch points. With such a method we could come up with something like the following:

- 20% of sales are for 100% attributable to our website
- 25% of sales are for 70% attributable to our website
- 15% of sales are for 50% attributable to our website

To make things a bit more challenging we may also come across websites that have a monetizing system incorporated but other financial goals also co-exist. Take for instance the example of a news site that offers ads within the site, a direct monetization of our visit based upon the news content they provide. For many news sites this ad revenue is a secondary goal as their major goal is a subscription for their online or off line newspaper. Here we will have to calculate with the direct income of ad revenue and combine it with an attribution of subscriptions.

Whatever the website and company we will encounter, we first have to look at the current money stream and the role our website and online strategy is playing within this stream. At the end we will come up with an amount in Dollars or Euro's that our website generates. This will give us the perfect starting point for assessing the strength of the 5 website value drivers. In essence what we have done is labeling our website with a money amount just like ecommerce sites provide. Great isn't it? Yes, it is, if our website plays a role in reaching money objectives. Luckily this is the case for many information-based websites especially for most company based websites although the challenge will be the attribution of profits and sales to these websites. But my experience tells me that in most cases we can come up with a workable attribution method. So when we will be able to attribute sales and profits to our website and online strategy we will have more or less the same starting point as we would have with an ecommerce website.

Okay, but what about websites that do not contribute to a financial goal? Or websites that do generate some cash but do not monetize their strengths in the most effective way? There are millions of these websites. What kind of websites are we talking about? Think of blogs or websites that do provide lots of free information about all sorts of topics. In some cases these websites generate cash through selling advertising space, in other cases they ask a non-committal contribution or they have some sponsors that will back some of the costs of running the website. A website like Wikipedia is a fine example where private donations keep it afloat. In general I will treat these websites alike. If some money is generated I will use it as a starting point before adding the 5 website value drivers. But I would not take the cash flow they amass in the same way as I would treat ecommerce websites or lead generating websites like most information based company websites are.

I will discuss the different treatment of these websites during the next phase when we will be adding the 5 website value drivers.

Phase 2: Financial valuation

As we have transformed our non-ecommerce website into a website with attributable results we are now able to use one of the financial valuation methods we have discussed in chapter 8. In general you could use one of the described methods but always be aware that within the attribution of results there are always more uncertainties than with ecommerce websites where attribution plays no role.

Phase 3: Assessing the strength of the 5 website value drivers

What role do the 5 website value drivers play with non-ecommerce websites? In general they play the same qualitative role but of course without the financial or money factor the role of these 5 drivers will become even more important. But by valuing an information based website with a fine financial attribution model we can overcome the lack of direct financial results.

In essence phase 3 is exactly the same as with ecommerce websites. As we have a financial value to start with we will just follow the qualitative method by adding weighting factors and assessing multipliers to come up with one estimated value for our website.

Maybe it is time to take a step back and take a look around to make sure we can make the distinctions between these different types of websites and their valuation method up to now.

So, let us summarize where we are at this moment.
1. We have dealt with ecommerce websites in the previous chapters. After we have valued the financial

results of an ecommerce website through one or more financial valuation methods we will apply a qualitative valuation by assessing the strength of the 5 website value drivers. In the end we will combine the results and we can come up with a value in your favorite currency. So that settles the ecommerce websites (sounds simple but of course the process will always be a challenge for your brains).

2. When we are dealing with a non-ecommerce website that generates leads that eventually lead to financial results we can use the same method as with ecommerce websites if (and that is important) we will be able to use a thorough attribution method of these results. Of course it will not be as perfect as the direct results an ecommerce website will show but in most cases it will present a workable method that let us use the same valuation method as with ecommerce websites. We will make a financial valuation and add the 5 website value drivers that will lead us to the value of our website or online strategy.

3. And what about websites that do not generate financial results? We will have to skip the first phase of our traditional method, that is the financial valuation. There are no hard figures available so we are left empty-handed. But that does not mean we cannot value such websites. How to handle this challenge? We start directly with phase 2. So we begin with analyzing the strengths and weaknesses of our 5 website value drivers. We will use weighting factors and give a qualitative appraisal of the relative strength of each website value driver. That leaves us with a qualitative analysis of our website. What is missing is the final value in a Dollar or Euro amount. We can stop there and learn from the insights we have garnered about

value generating factors of our website. An interesting study to say the least, but that is not what this book is about. What we really want is a value in a sum of money. To accomplish that we will add a third entity in this process, the possible buyer.

To summarize the valuation process: Up to now we have used a quantitative financial valuation process if financial results are available (ecommerce websites) and attributable (non-ecommerce websites that generate attributable results). After that we have used the qualitative valuation process by appraising the 5 website value drivers. In the end a single value can be labeled when we combine the quantitative and qualitative results by using weighting factors and multipliers (as we have seen in the former chapters).

But when no financial results are available we cannot use this method. What we will be able to do is adding the possible buyer.

B] The possible buyer method

Our goal is to come up with a global website valuation for websites without any direct or attributable financial results. As we have no money value to work with we will need to transform the intrinsic values of our website (the 5 website value drivers) into a money value. To do this we turn things topsy-turvy. We will add a market oriented approach to the process. Our basic question will be: What would our website be worth for a possible buyer? The answer to this question lies within the solutions our website provides to the problems a buyer is seeking to solve.

In other terms: what kind of value is our website adding to the business model of a possible buyer?

This value will be found in one or more of our website value drivers.
It could be our strength in organic traffic that would benefit a possible buyer, it could be our online authority or maybe the way we promote our website (although that would probably not be the case with a non-ecommerce or non-attributable website). In most cases it is the organic strength and online authority that will be the assets a possible buyer is looking for in websites that do not garner financial results.

Before we will dive into the ways we can discover these values and turn them into a Dollar or Euro amount I want to emphasize that this approach is not only feasible to websites that do not convert traffic in any money amount. There are numerous websites or blogs that do have some monetization in place. Think of using AdSense or placing some banners. If you would only calculate with the money amount the sale of advertising space will fetch you could be underselling yourself.

What would be the worth of Wikipedia based solely upon the revenue it generates through donations offered by its supporters? Would it be more if an advertising model was being used? Or would it even be better when other revenue models would be applied? A complex question as adding different earnings models would alter the value it would add to users and even search engines. You could win on one side and loose on the other. This will often be the case when a website would be used in another commercial way by a new owner. Still, that does not limit us to take on the exercise. That leaves us with the question how to go about doing just that?

What would a possible buyer be willing to pay?
I have to admit that we are entering a somewhat unknown territory. That is why I would use this approach only when there is no or insufficient financial data available. That being said, although our exercise will be surrounded by ifs and buts we are not completely empty-handed. We have our website value drivers' strengths and weaknesses mapped out and our

human intelligence to cope with the challenge. That leaves us with the central question: What would our website be worth from the perspective of a possible buyer? To answer this question it is good to notice that there are different buying parties out there with different objectives for buying a non-ecommerce website. Let's examine some motives of possible buyers:

1. **Buyers that are in it for the organic traffic**
   Organic traffic is free traffic, we all know this, but off course it is not true. To generate lots of organic traffic you must have the right content that attracts people searching on the internet but that is only the simple explanation. Established website domains, engaging content, an active content marketing strategy, building authority, years of hard work, it will eventually lead to a vast flow of organic traffic flow. In short, it takes time, energy and money to build this organic base. Moreover, organic traffic is often high converting traffic. It is no small wonder that organic traffic is a precious asset sought for by many online businesses. Instead of building it yourself slowly and painfully a website acquisition may be the fast ticket to get "free" traffic within your sales funnel.

2. **Buyers that look for new markets**
   Instead of expanding your market scope by adding new product categories to your existing portfolio you may choose to skip the process of building a reputation and trying to get the attention and interest of new target groups. Buying a company that services the markets you are after may be an option but if your main focus is online why not look for 1 or more websites without having to buy a complete company. You only have to tweak the right target audience into consumers. A process of course that will cause some headaches before it delivers the sought after results. But it may take less aspirins than other options.

3. **Getting access to other website's authority**
   Suppose you are the proud owner of an ecommerce website that sells women's clothing. Your online shop is state of the art, your products are great and your margins are solid. But somehow your sales could use a boost. Wouldn't it be great if you could incorporate that highly popular fashion blog within your marketing strategy? You will not expect to turn all these fashion blog followers into regular customers but you would be able to gently promote your brand within this blog. In the long term your ecommerce brand will benefit from it hugely, if done properly.

There are many more reasons why third parties would be interested in the acquisition of a non-ecommerce website. The challenge lies in putting a price label on the motives of a possible buyer. As we said before the value of a non-ecommerce website lies in most cases within your organic traffic strength or online authority strength. But how to gauge the value of these relative strengths with the eyes of a possible buyer?
There are several methods to do that. Let's discuss them:

Estimating the worth of your organic traffic

Organic traffic has a value, that is no surprise, but it differs among certain denominators what price tag you could add to it. In general you could say that the more a website caters to a specific target audience the more worth your traffic has. And then it depends on the vertical or niche a website is operating in. Organic traffic from a fashion blog has a lower value than organic traffic from a financial blog. How can you estimate the worth of your organic traffic?
I use the following methods:

1. **Gauge the eCPC**
   The eCPC or Effective Cost Per Click will be the expected return your traffic would generate when you

would sell your traffic to online advertisers. It would be the return you make when for instance you would use Google AdSense on your website. Beware that eCPC has a dual explanation, one with the eyes of the publisher as we will use it and one with the eye of the advertiser (how much would the advertiser has to pay per click when one would advertise on your site). eCPC's may be calculated by estimating Click Through Rates and Cost Per Clicks. CPC's can be obtained by looking at the average Cost Per Click a platform like Google Ads will charge to advertisers. Of course, the major drawback here is that we only concentrate on the worth of traffic that is used in advertising. Maybe a possible buyer has a better than average return and margin on the stuff they are selling and then the calculation would offer an undervalued estimate.

2. **Calculate with CPC's only**

A simpler method is to concentrate on average CPC's only. You could look at average CPC's in advertising on Google Ads or other platforms to be able to put a price on your organic traffic. The discussion will be whether to use CPC's from Search or Display campaigns as there is a major difference between someone who is actively searching for what you have to offer or someone who is interested in your topic but not willing to make a transaction. In some cases you could use a CPC somewhere in between as traffic from a very specific blog or website has more value than the average websites that Display campaigns target. As you know, most Display campaigns put ads on not so relevant websites or even non-relevant websites based upon the expected interest of a wide target group.

3. **Estimate conversion rates**

Would your non-ecommerce organic traffic easily being transformed into buying traffic? Many factors will impact the question to that answer. The more your organic traffic is really interested in products or services you are offering (company websites) or talking about (blogs) the more positive your answer will be. Taking it a bit further: What conversion rate would your traffic generate within the same topic of your website but within a lead generating or ecommerce environment? This estimation will be a challenge but when looking at conversion rates within your vertical it may supply the answer.

4. **Benchmarking**
   What did a similar website like yours fetch when being sold? That could give you an idea about the worth of your information based website. Benchmarking is also important in supplying answers to the above mentioned methods in trying to get average market CPC's or conversion rates. One drawback: it is not always easy to obtain information about sold websites. Make it 2 drawbacks: comparing different websites without having access to all data is even more difficult.

Estimating the worth of your online authority

Adding a multiplier to online authority when gauging the strength of it is one thing but putting a value directly on online authority without any additional financial data is much harder. But there is a way to help us out.

As we have said before, some possible buyers are predominantly looking for online authority. They know that it is a strong driver of consumer behavior, an influential asset to get your hands on. We have seen how to gauge the relative strength of online authority. We have to use the same approach here and of course the result will be essentially qualitative, not quantitative. How to quantify this outcome? Will that be possible? I can tell you what I would do. As online authority always has a strong impact on organic traffic I combine these 2 value drivers.

I would make a qualitative estimation in the same way as we would handle the relative strength of the website value driver online authority. The result will be a multiplier. Then I will follow the exercise mentioned above about valuing our organic traffic (in most cases by using an eCPC or CPC approach). By doing that I can use the multiplier of online authority on the organic traffic value estimation.

It would lead to:

Money amount online traffic value x Multiplier online authority strength

I hope you are still with me. To be honest, it may sound a bit complicated all these different approaches and methods. But I have good news for you, we now have a complete valuation method for both ecommerce and non-ecommerce websites. So, generally we are done. To make it even a bit simpler I will summarize the whole systematic approach in the next chapter.

Chapter 11: Flow chart website valuation

In the former chapters I introduced a website valuation method for ecommerce websites and non-ecommerce websites. The latter group I divided into websites with attributable financial results and websites that do not generate financial results or negligible results. That completes the whole website valuation process. I think it is time to present a simple flow chart for each valuation method because after reading these different methods and approaches you could be a bit confused (although I do not underestimate your deductive strength).

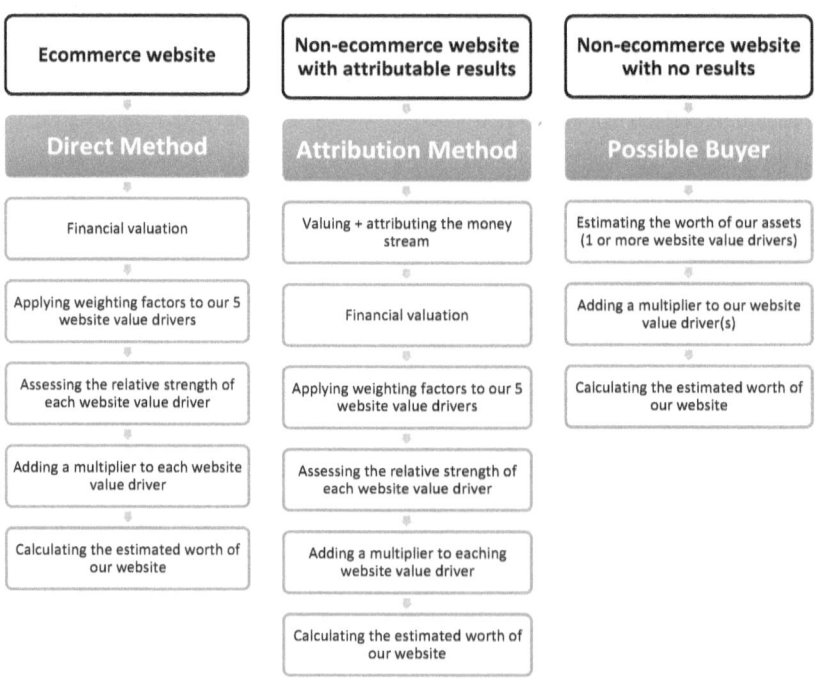

In essence we have now covered the whole process depending on what kind of website we are valuing. Of course, this only describes the method. In practice you will come across many challenges and choices to make. Like I have said before, it is never a straightforward mathematical process that will eventually lead to a 100% bulletproof result. Valuations are never bulletproof, they will remain estimations of future results propelled backwards.

To add to the difficulties of website valuation there are some pitfalls to avoid. In the next chapter I will get into some of these pitfalls you may come across when valuing a website.

Chapter 12: Pitfalls of website valuations

I have said it before, valuing a website is not a simple task with a clear-cut outcome. The end result will always be an estimation and the process of getting to that estimation will absorb a good part of your brain power. To make things even more tempting, there are some extra pitfalls you want to avoid. Here I will discuss a few of them.

Pitfall 1: Bot traffic

When analyzing data from Analytics or other statistical packages you might think that you are viewing real data stemming from clicks and ultimately originating from human interaction. Alas, that is not always the case. A part of the traffic might come from bots or computers. In some cases bot traffic is easily spotted. You may see loads of traffic coming from 1 IP address and filtering by country may also give a good idea. There are some countries that excel in sending out bots to websites from all over the world.

Unfortunately, there is also bot traffic that you cannot see right away. You will only notice it when some recurring patterns become clear. I myself had to deal once with computerized traffic stemming from an advertising platform that went a bit further than click fraud. Normally you would expect that click fraud happens on an incoming website or search engine and the traffic on your website generating from this fraud would be of very low quality indeed. Here it was different, traffic from click fraud was seemingly of high quality. Several pages were visited and it also clicked on ads run by this website. The result was incoming click fraud and outgoing click fraud. The owner of the website had no idea that this was taking place. Only when the receiving party of the ads run by this owner began complaining about quality issues things became clear.

But the true crime was committed by incoming traffic to this website originating from ad click fraud bots.

How to look for bot traffic? Go through your traffic reports, dig deeper into sources and websites, especially referral traffic and paid traffic. Go through your country lists, dig deeper into cities and sometimes you will see that many website visitors all live in a tiny place in the middle of nowhere.

Pitfall 2: Paid traffic

We already have talked about click fraud but here I want to warn you for another pitfall that concerns paid traffic. It is a bit more complicated and not easy to notice right away. To illustrate what I am talking about I will use our fictitious online shop that is selling sneakers. Running a search advertising campaign on important keywords like "sneakers for sale" or "new Adidas sneakers" will attract relevant traffic to your website. Unfortunately this traffic comes at a price. CPC's will be high. But keywords like "measuring foot size" have much lower CPC's. Unfortunately conversions are almost non-existent. When you would look at average CPC's you might conclude that this website is running a very effective campaign as it has a lower than average CPC. But don't give it an A level for that unless you have considered conversion rates.

Taking it a step further, in display traffic things might confuse you still more. CPC's from display campaigns are always considerably lower than search campaign CPC's. Especially when one is triggering much more traffic from display than from search this might set you on the wrong foot, although in most cases you can filter this out very nicely (especially traffic coming from Google Ads). The main concern however is display traffic coming from untagged sources. This could be traffic coming from banners placed directly at blogs or other platforms that do not offer auto-tagging. Then you will have to go through your referral traffic and discern real referral traffic from paid "referral" traffic.

In most cases there is no malicious intent on part of the selling party. It is just a thing that may occur and you will have to look into.

Pitfall 3: Iceberg websites

Never heard of it, did you? Right, I invented the name myself. This is one of the trickiest things you could encounter. And sometimes it is a deliberate way of fooling a possible buyer. But you can also say that the buying party needs to take responsibility in its own hands and investigate what one is buying.

What are we talking about? An iceberg website is a website that appears to be active in 1 competitive theme but below the surface it attracts traffic that is not interested in this (mostly highly competitive) theme. What it does is appearing to be a shiny jewel in a particular market but the actual role in this market is blown up. I call it an iceberg website as one shields the base of most of the traffic from the public eye. The shiny iceberg glistens in the sun but underneath there is a large base of just frozen water.

Let's discuss an example. Say you are running a website in the insurance business. You operate a blog where you discuss different insurance products and people can compare rates and discuss personal experiences with insurance companies and agencies. As you will know, Pay Per Clicks in the insurance business are extremely high and a very popular insurance blog with loads of traffic could be worth a considerable sum. Generating traffic in this industry however is also a major challenge. So what do you do? You think it may be easier to attract traffic that is not looking for insurance products. You will write blogs on other subjects or you run website fora on a range of different topics. On the surface however you still appear as an insurance blog, you have no internal links to these other pages that attract traffic.

Sounds far-fetched you think? Well, I know several websites that operate just like that. Not in the insurance industry but in other industries. I personally have never dealt with these types of websites but I know from websites that have been sold for millions that were attracting the bulk of their traffic from other topics than the one they claim. But how is this possible? If you would look a little deeper into Analytics you will notice this, or not? Well, it may be a bit tricky. Suppose you run many website fora where discussions about your general theme and many irrelevant themes are going on. URL's may be made dynamic so within Analytics you will not notice this easily. You really have to dig into the website itself and compare this with Analytics data.

The most vulnerable market for iceberg websites is the media industry. They sell ads to advertisers based upon buyer persona's, target markets and market reach. Ultimately it is the advertiser that will lose. As an advertiser you might think your ad is shown to a large and relevant target group but in fact your ads will appear to a large irrelevant target group. But as a buying media company you would not want to pay for traffic that is irrelevant for the market you want to invest in. In the end advertisers add the numbers and they stop paying top dollar for a media outlet that does not bring in conversions. So, beware for online icebergs, they may sink you.

Pitfall 4: Financial results

As our website valuation starts with a financial valuation it goes without saying that the financial results you will have to deal with should be bullet proof. Well, they aren't always what they appear to be. That is why I strongly recommend to work with an official accountant that is bound to supply the data you will need. Also beware of financial predictions just like future cash flows and sales. Looking back to predict the future is always a bit tricky even when historical data seems to point solidly towards an almost certain outcome. That being said, in our business we cannot avoid the process of extrapolation. When all parties acknowledge the uncertainty that is surrounding this process, future disappointment might be prevented.

Pitfall 5: Pressure from your client

To make things simple: a seller wants a high selling price, a buyer wants a low purchase price. In most cases a website appraiser will be hired by one of these parties. That may tempt an appraiser to please one's customer. Even when no explicit pressure is exercised an appraiser might be tempted to sympathize with the client that ultimately will pay the bill. How to avoid this? Of course by keeping an objective state of mind. But it depends on the role you play. If your function is to value a website and that valuation will be put on the table in negotiations than an absolute objectivity is required. If however, you are asked to give your opinion as an adviser for one of the parties involved your role may vary. You even may act as one of the negotiators on behalf of your client. Than your role is completely different, but always make clear what your role is to your client and the other party involved.

There are many more pitfalls that will present themselves while valuing a website. This is not a simple and straightforward line of business. You can compare it to a merger and acquisition process. In fact valuing websites will become more important in the M&A business where hectic situations, time pressure and vast interests will come together.

Chapter 13: What about the value of domains?

Somehow there has always been a thriving market for buying and selling web domains. In the early years of the internet (between 1998 and 2003) acquiring single keyword domains seemed a great way of investing in the future development of the internet. The reasoning behind this acquisition spree was that single keyword domains would attract organic traffic easily and obtaining a catchy, easy to remember domain name would always be worth a certain amount of money. In essence this reasoning was justified, in these early years organic traffic and domain names were positively correlated. That meant that even a low quality website with the right keyword domain name could attract considerable flows of organic traffic.

I must admit that I myself also registered many domains and I even bought some domains at a considerable sum from domain traders. After some years I unloaded the bulk of these domains by just stopping registration fees. They were worthless to sell and too costly to hold. Some of these domains however proved a smart investment as I made websites out of them or used them in link building (another leftover from the good old days).

As the internet developed search engines altered algorithms in a way that website content and quality became much more important. Having a keyword domain with a low content website does not bring you traffic anymore. But a catchy name containing the main keyword theme of your business still can prove its worth. That brings us to the following question: How to value a website domain?

The worth of empty domains without a website

An empty domain without a website is worth what a buyer is willing to pay for it, it's as simple as that. There is no way to value such domains. Even if the domain contains a high volume keyword within a competitive market you cannot make a solid valuation of such a domain. It will not automatically attract organic traffic so going on that path will lead you nowhere. But of course, if you build a great website on this domain and you will be patient it may prove its worth. But telling you upfront what this worth may be is mere speculation. Mind, there are numerous domain extensions out there and a domain with a high volume keyword will probably be registered many times around in different extensions so you will never be unique.

The worth of a domain with a website built around

In some cases you will come across website domains that do function as a website. The owner has put website content on this domain in order to let traffic build. This may be a good strategy. In order to value such a domain/website you will have more to work with. There is traffic coming in and search engines have given it a place in search engine results pages. But still, it will be a difficult task. Generally the website content of such a domain is not on the level of active websites that compete within the same market. If a possible buyer wants to use the domain in competing in a certain market it may save some time in getting the website off the ground. Especially when it is an old domain this will be an advantage. The famous Google Sandbox will be by-passed.

In general the worth of web domains is diminishing as search engines are predominantly focused on website content. Of course, a well to remember web domain may help you in marketing your website but starting a website from scratch may be the better option. You may have to wait a while before search engines will pick you up (the Sandbox effect) but you will not run the risk of buying a domain that has somehow gotten a bad reputation in the past (it might be used in link building or far worse black hat SEO strategies). But in some cases a web domain may provide the best alternative. After all, it all depends on your strategy and goals.

Chapter 14: Websites as online real estate

As I have said in the beginning of this book, I consider websites as online real estate. A website must be built , it needs care and maintenance and it may be bought or sold. Above all, it has a value of its own and in most cases that value can be calculated.

Up to now most stakeholders do not treat websites as online real estate. A website owner may regard it as a marketing instrument, the company accountant may see it as expenses and even investors do not look upon it as an asset. But in essence, a website is exactly that, an asset. In my opinion these views will change, rapidly. Let's discuss the concept of online real estate for different website types and viewed from all angles for different stakeholders.

Ecommerce websites vs physical shops

So, what's the difference? Of course we can come up with many differences between a physical and online shop but what it all boils down to is that a shop is a place where you can buy stuff, whether it be online or off line. For a shopkeeper a shop is a means to do business. Most shopkeepers rent the physical shop they need to sell their stuff, in most cases they own the online shop they need to do their ecommerce business. Physical shops are seen as assets and they are treated that way by investors, real estate owners, accountants and the local tax authorities. Why would we treat online shops differently? I see no reason why.

An ecommerce website is not a leaflet and it is not a catalogue. The last distinction is important. Some people still regard ecommerce websites as online catalogues. Direct sales through catalogues used to be a popular marketing and sales model up to the beginning of the new millennium. It is true that this direct sales model has large similarities with the online ecommerce model. But there are important distinctions between the two. The catalogue by itself was not sufficient to make the sale, you also would need a sales team to collect the orders by telephone or traditional mail. Another big difference is that this catalogue was distributed only to the addresses you had sent it to in the first place. The catalogue itself did not attract new potential customers outside its circulation that were triggered by its contents. In contrast, ecommerce websites do attract customers that are triggered by website content. With an ecommerce website a complete customer journey may be fulfilled. Attention, Interest, Desire and Action, all stages will be performed and fulfilled by the ecommerce website. In the end a complete and paid order will be processed. So, indeed it does exactly what a physical shop does. So, let's treat it like it is. It is an asset for the owner and a marketing and sales instrument for the shopkeeper or merchant. It does not matter whether merchant and owner are the same entities, that is also common in the physical shop world. Moreover we are seeing the same evolution online as in the physical world where ownership and retailing are parting. Look at the success of online platforms like Amazon and Alibaba. They are online shopping malls where shopkeepers rent space. No one will disagree of these shops being world class assets.

Non-ecommerce websites vs commercial real estate

Commercial real estate is a broad term that comprises all sorts of real estate with a commercial use. Think of office buildings, industrial property, hotels, warehouses and of course shopping buildings. I already made a case for ecommerce websites to be treated like online real estate. But can we put the same label on non-ecommerce websites? I think we can but I have to make an exception for empty web domains.

Why exclude empty web domains? Because they do not function as real estate. They do not attract visitors, they cannot hold visitors and they add no value on their own. Only when being operated they will come to fruition. Couldn't we treat empty domains as building sites? That is a tempting one, but I do not see it that way. A building site possesses a value depended upon its location and the permit to build a specific commercial unit on it. A domain is an empty shell with no guarantees of success nor transferrable rights to be exploited.

So that leaves us with a whole bunch of information based websites like blogs and news sites as well as company websites that offer product information and /or website content based upon the markets they serve. Will these non-ecommerce websites pass the test of online real estate? I think they do.

The essence of commercial real estate is its commercial driven functionality. It is a facilitator of commercial activity. It offers space to perform a job (office space) or acts as a market place for buyers and sellers (shopping malls, stores, supermarkets), offers accommodation (hotels and restaurants) or acts as a place to meet or discover (public libraries, museums, theaters). Whatever its function, its purpose is not the building itself but the activity it accommodates.

How does that compare to company websites? These websites also facilitate a commercial function: interaction between the company products or services and its target audience. Although these websites do not realize direct sales they do produce leads and interactions with potential customers. You could make the point that these websites are merely part of the company marketing effort and of course this is also true. But they are more than advertisements, catalogues or leaflets. They act as an entity on their own in attracting new visitors and driving new leads based upon their position in search engines and their ability to generate interest and action through their website appeal. You could say that a company website is like a commercial outlet, an extra showroom that enables you to receive people interested in your proposition, to let them browse around your products and services, get to know you through your stories and interact with them by chat, mail or phone.

And what about blogs and other information websites? They also attract people that are interested in your stories and news items. You will show them ads to make a living and maybe you will charge them a subscription fee. In essence these are commercial activities that come to fruition after interaction with your audiences. Again you could make a true comment saying that a blog is just the equivalent of a physical newspaper or magazine. In a way that is true but a website is more than a paper magazine. Physical newspapers only are distributed to their subscribers or they are being sold in newsstands. They do not have the ability to drive readers on their own (only when passed through but that is not the same).

It is this traffic engine that makes a website unique. It will take up space in the online shopping streets of search engines and they will pop up through links on other websites. Every single website occupies a place on this web of commercial streets on the internet. They are just like physical shops in a gigantic shopping mall that attracts people's interest, enables them to enter your online space and interact with them.

The implications of regarding websites as online real estate

Why do I make such a fuss about treating websites as online real estate? Because I think websites in general are underrated. In today's world a large part of human interaction starts on the internet and in more and more cases it will end there as well by performing a task or purchasing the item that one needs. The part that off line real estate played in our lives up to just a few years ago has been replaced by online activities. We do not need to go to the shopping mall to see "what's in store". We do not need to go out to meet people in café's or on the streets and we do not need to go to a showroom to be informed about the newest car model. That sounds a bit gloomy but I myself do not see it that way. Online interaction is not the end of human interaction. It only takes up another form of interaction. But this is not the place to discuss the pros and cons of the internet.

So why call it online real estate? Because a website is an asset that resembles the function physical real estate played in our world before the internet. Treating a website as an asset instead of an expense has major implications. Here I discuss some of these implications viewed from the different stakeholders that are involved.

1. **Impact on business owners and general management**
   By regarding websites as online real estate decisions about online strategy will move up higher in the company hierarchy. The cost of building and operating a website will no longer be viewed as marketing expenses but as company investments. It will also result in a more strategic and long term approach to online activities. I think this is needed. There are still too many companies that regard their website as just a channel of communication. But it is the place where the customer journey begins and (in many cases) will end. It is the core of their business and it is an investment in the future of one's company.

2. **Impact on accounting and taxation**

My point here is not only to call websites company assets but to really deal with them as such on company balance sheets. In my opinion each and every ecommerce website should be put under assets and not be put within the profit and loss account. In general I would do the same with company websites and information based websites but here I would give much leeway to each different company depended upon the role of its website within the company as a whole.

What will be the effects of putting ecommerce websites as assets on balance sheets? It will make the worth of a website visible to all stakeholders including investors and owners. It also will make things easier when new capital is needed or in cases of buying out shareholders or in events of transferring ownership of a company.

It also will impact the way a company will be taxed. Direct write offs of costs through the profit and loss account will not be as easy anymore. There must be made distinctions between website expenses and website investments. It also will need a solid depreciation system to rightly adhere a price tag on a website during its predicted life span. I am the first to admit that this will have large implications for accounting and taxation but I think we should take this step to be consistent about the way we administer the way we operate a business.

3. **Impact on investments and investors**

   Investing in a company is above all investing in its assets. In my opinion this calls for a proper list of assets clearly communicated through the company's balance sheet. Will adding an ecommerce website inflate the balance sheet? In most cases it will, although the name "inflate" is not the right word here. It will add value where it should be added. In some cases it may have implications on the worth of shares or stocks owned in a particular company. It may also have an impact on lending capacity. That sounds all a bit tricky but it is not. Forgetting to list a building a company owns would be the same mistake as just not mentioning the value of the ecommerce site a company owns. It is as simple as that. Will a company be worth more if the value of an ecommerce website is added to the balance sheet? In general, the answer will be yes. But again, that is not inflating the balance sheet, it is correcting a mistake from the past. Before you should think otherwise. What are investors in Alibaba and Amazon paying for? They pay for their assets and their assets are their websites (apart from other activities they manage such as cloud services). Investors will gain understanding and transparency when website assets are properly listed within the balance sheet.

So, let's call websites and particular ecommerce sites what they really are: online real estate. Treat them accordingly and all stakeholders will have a more accurate picture of your business.

Chapter 15: Acquiring a website

Considering the acquisition of a website the first you will notice is that you will be entering a new world where little information is to be found. Here I will give you some things to think about as selling a website may be an adventure but acquiring one will be a challenge.

1. Browse through some website market places

There are some online platforms that act as a market place for websites. Flippa, Empire Flippers and Exchange are 3 examples. Most of the websites offered on these platforms are predominantly centered around websites with low to medium price ranges. You will also come across many drop shipping websites and affiliate websites. You will learn something about prices and the information these sellers offer. All information is useful so register yourself on these platforms and go through some of the details. But never forget, the prices you will see vary greatly and the same can be said about the quality and strength of these websites. You will leave these platforms with as much puzzlement as you entered them (and even more). That being said, I do think that these platforms are the right place to start your journey and they may even be the place to buy a reasonably priced website.

2. Large acquisitions require a team of specialists

You will really have to go through all available data and look for possible pitfalls. That requires the advice of a very seasoned online marketing specialist. You will also need a good financial specialist that is able to calculate historic financial data and extrapolate results. You may seek the advice of a web designer that will go through the technical stuff of the website. What you really need is a good team and in most cases you will not find all these specialists within your company. In fact I strongly advice an outside opinion. I know of some large acquisitions that were carried out in-house and they overpaid for websites they didn't know enough of. Do not make this mistake!

3. Discuss your plans before acquisition

What do you want with that other website? What are your plans? Would the alternative of setting up a website on your won be a better one? There are multiple questions to be asked BEFORE buying a website. Discuss your plans with your management team, outside advisors and think and ponder before getting out your purse.

4. Work on your newly acquired website

Do not think that in buying a website you can sit back and smell the roses. The real work will start just now. Maybe you will have to alter some webpages, be sure that you do not throw away the engine pages of the website you just bought. But above all, make sure you will work on your newly acquired website, build, expand, enlarge. Do not sit on your website, work on it! That's the way to add more value to your website and get the best return of your investment. This all sound obvious maybe, but I have seen so many websites that were almost abandoned after acquisition, a real shame!

5. Make your own calculations regarding the asking price

The seller of a website stipulates its price but you must do the math. Before negotiating you will need to know what price would be justified. So dig into the data and start appraising.

Even if a valuation has been made by the selling party make your own one. Never forget, buying a website is much more complicated than buying real estate. There are no fixed figures regarding prices per square meter or location bonuses. You will need to go through the nitty gritty of all components that make up the value of a website (and after reading this book you know what we are talking about).

6. Negotiate with knowledge

After really examining the website you want to acquire you will not only gain the needed insights in deciding whether to pursue the acquisition or not. You may also use this knowledge in the actual negotiations and deal making. It will most certainly make the deal a better one. You may want to hire an outside specialist that will support you in negotiations based upon his or her knowledge in the field.

7. There is no certainty in acquisitions

You don't want to hear this warning. But obviously it is true. The future is always uncertain. The value of a website that has been calculated prudently may not materialize. There may be oversights, the market may change, competition may gear up, the economy may go down, even political decisions may cast a shadow on future sales and profits. The list goes on and on, uncertainty is something we will have to live with. In essence, do not blame others, do not blame yourself, it is just a fact of life, so live with it and make the best out of it. That being said, ask and expect that everyone involved performs the task at hand with great care and diligence.

Chapter 16: The future of retailing and website acquisitions

In this last chapter I will share some personal thoughts about the future of online retailing, website transactions and website valuations. We are entering a phase in the evolution of the internet that is comparable to phases we have seen before in off line retailing. Mergers and acquisitions of online shops and platforms will become more and more popular as competition will grow.

1. An acquisition driven market

Maybe you wonder why I am talking more about acquiring a website than selling one, especially in these last 2 chapters. The answer is that the market is driven by acquisitions.
Instead of building a website on your own we will see more website acquisitions especially in ecommerce websites.
Online retailers will have to make choices about expanding their markets. What to do? Add new products for new markets to existing ecommerce sites, build a new ecommerce site from scratch or acquiring an ecommerce website that already has a proven track record. The last option is a tempting one, especially if you have a workable plan on the table. You can alter the acquired website to your design and market strategy and add a proven strategy for growth. It all makes sense. Just look back at the off line world of retailing some 10 – 20 years ago. Then we saw the same wave of mergers and acquisitions in retailing land. But acquiring a brick and mortar store is a much bigger challenge than acquiring an online store. On the internet you can tweak and reshape an acquired shop much easier than you can do with a physical store where location and street traffic are fixed factors you will have to deal with.

2. The impact of the Amazon's and Alibaba's of this world

"In 10 years' time there will be no individual online stores left. Everybody will buy at Amazon and Alibaba". I heard someone saying that and people were nodding their heads in awe and approval. Let me be clear about this: I love what Amazon and Alibaba and a whole bunch of other online platforms have brought to this world. I am in awe too. But although they have a huge impact on online shopping they will never be able to stop the growth of specialized online shops. True, they raise the bar for perfect order processing and pricing. However, a well-managed online shop will be able to offer a similar proposition. Another thing to consider: most products you will find on Multi Sided Platforms like Amazon and Alibaba are supplied by third party retailers and traders. Adding the platform is 1 link more in the supply chain. So pricewise there is not a particular advantage, only order execution may be swifter and cheaper but that puts pressure on the mix of products. Fast turnover is the holy grail in cheap and swift processing and this means that more product variations with less market demand will be ousted from the process (or made more expensive to hold and promote for third parties on these platforms).

Looking back in time we saw the advent and growth of department stores in the 50s, 60s and 70s of last century and their subsequent decline in the 80s and 90s when specialized stores took control of shopping streets. Will the same happen with online platforms? Not necessarily, but I do think that some platforms will grow out of touch with customers. And in the meanwhile direct online shops will grow in strength and performance. One of the reasons for that will be economies of scale realized by mergers and acquisitions.

3. The future of online retailing

In the coming 5 to 20 years I foresee huge competition between platforms (the battle Amazon – Alibaba will be a fierce one) and between individual online shops competing within the same markets. I will also see online conglomerates taking shape. These conglomerates will consist of several online shops competing on different markets but operated by the same management and order processing system. For outsiders they make look as platforms but without the multi sided approach (no third party sales).

Online retailing will become more and more a battle for optimization and a winner-takes-all approach. The online shopping street will be controlled by parties that will be able to offer the best products for the best prices brought to your doorstep in the most efficient and fast way. Small individual shops must be careful. They will have to operate in the niches left over by the big ones or get together and form a powerhouse on their own.

4. And what about physical stores and omni channel strategies?

Is the end of physical stores near? I don't think so, but our familiar shopping street will change. There will be less physical stores but better ones. Large physical stores make place for smaller specialty stores. And there will be more space occupied by fine restaurants, craftsmanship stores and taste-and-experience centers. The large physical retail chains and formulas will become more and more online orientated and here too an acquisition strategy will become a popular alternative for expanding one's own online formula. Omnichannel will remain but I do think that the online component will eventually become dominant over the physical one.

5. The evolution of the market for website valuations

All the above mentioned scenarios lead to more market consolidations. Ecommerce thrives on optimization of all processes and optimization thrives on scale and volume. The more data, the faster you can improve and the easier you can smart out your competitor. This all will lead to managing large scale online operations. The fastest way to get there is by acquiring other ecommerce sites or platforms. Of course that will also spark the market for website valuations. What an expanding market for website acquisitions needs is a well-established way of valuing a website and its subsequent online strategy.

6. Changing the M&A market

The global Mergers & Acquisitions market comprises a myriad of consultancy firms that are traditionally focused on companies and physical assets. The online component of businesses however is rising rapidly and the same can be said about pure online companies that exploit websites, ecommerce websites and online platforms. M&A deals will be more and more concentrated around the online part of companies. This will shake up the composition of the M&A team where the need for specific online specialists will rise exponentially. It will also change the way mergers and acquisitions take place. Traditionally M&A's concentrate on deals within the same market or vertical. In the coming years we will see more cross-market acquisitions. That has everything to do with the art of online marketing and growing an online business. When processes are in place it doesn't matter whether one is selling or shipping clothes, computers or sunglasses.

Use your brain power!

I have come to the end of this book. I hope you have enjoyed reading it although I must confess that joy wasn't the goal I set. What I really wanted to do is to introduce a way of valuing a website and let you think about what makes up the worth of a website. I have introduced the 5 website value drivers and a structural method of website valuation. That does not mean that there may be different ways to come up with a proper calculation of the worth of a website. Eventually I think several methods will co-exist. That does not matter. What does matter is that you must include all parts that make up the worth of a website. What also matters is your mindset. When trying to come up with a value of a website you will have to see through all the data and decide what will contribute more or less to future results. To be able to do that you may rely on all sorts of calculations, extrapolations, qualifications, tools, statistics and forecasts. But what it ultimately boils down is using your brain power.

Forget artificial intelligence, what the world really needs is clear and creative thinking. We need YOU!

Thanks for reading. I really appreciate the time you invested to let my thoughts enter yours. Now it's up to you to decide what to do with it and bring it to another level. I wish you all the best.

www.ingramcontent.com/pod-product-compliance
Lightning Source LLC
Chambersburg PA
CBHW031418210526
45464CB00005B/1949